Philadelphia Area Cemeteries

Allan M. Heller

4880 Lower Valley Road, Atglen, PA 19310 USA

Library of Congress Cataloging-in-Publication
Data

Heller, Allan M.
  Philadelphia area cemeteries / by Allan M. Heller.
    p. cm.
  ISBN 0-7643-2222-2 (pbk.)
  1. Cemeteries—Pennsylvania—Philadelphia
Region—History. 2. Philadelphia Region (Pa.)—
History, Local. 3. Philadelphia Region (Pa.)—
Buildings, structures, etc. 4. Philadelphia Region
(Pa.)—Biography. I. Title.

F158.61.A1H45 2005
974.8'1—dc22
                                    2005002776

Designed by Mark David Bowyer
Type set in Lydian BT/Souvenir Lt BT

ISBN: 0-7643-2222-2
Printed in China

Published by Schiffer Publishing Ltd.
4880 Lower Valley Road
Atglen, PA 19310
Phone: (610) 593-1777; Fax: (610) 593-2002
E-mail: Info@schifferbooks.com

For the largest selection of fine reference books on this
and related subjects, please visit our web site at
www.schifferbooks.com
We are always looking for people to write books on
new and related subjects. If you have an idea for a
book please contact us at the above address.

This book may be purchased from the publisher.
Include $3.95 for shipping.
Please try your bookstore first.
You may write for a free catalog.

In Europe, Schiffer books are distributed by
Bushwood Books
6 Marksbury Ave.
Kew Gardens
Surrey TW9 4JF England
Phone: 44 (0) 20 8392-8585; Fax: 44 (0) 20 8392-
9876
E-mail: info@bushwoodbooks.co.uk
Free postage in the U.K., Europe; air mail at cost.

Contents

Introduction

Beneath those rugged elms, that yew-tree's shade,
Where heaves the turf in many a mouldering heap,
Each in his narrow cell forever laid,
The rude forefathers of the hamlet sleep.
– Thomas Gray, Elegy Written in a Country Churchyard.

In November of 1682, William Penn founded the counties of Bucks, Chester, and Philadelphia, and became the official proprietor and first governor of the colony of Pennsylvania. The vast 40,000 square miles, which comprised approximately the present boundaries of the commonwealth, had been granted to Penn a year earlier by the English king Charles II, in lieu of 16,000 pounds owed to Penn's late father. The name "Pennsylvania," Greek for "Penn's Woods," was suggested by the British monarch as a tribute to William Penn senior, a prominent admiral. At that time, the tri-county region was populated largely by Swedes, Dutch, and English, who traded furs and other goods with the Lenni Lenape Indians.

Penn, a convert to the Quaker faith, sought to establish a society based on personal and religious freedom. Quakers in England faced growing persecution, and Penn himself was imprisoned numerous times. Philadelphia, the first county seat, soon rivaled New York in prestige and population. Thousands followed in the wake of Penn's exodus, seeking both tolerance and prosperity, branching westward in what was to become the second state 105 years later.

As decades turn to centuries, a society that takes so much for granted has all but forgotten those who forged the future of not only Pennsylvania, but the entire nation. We walk oblivious in their footsteps, enjoy the liberties that many of them died to preserve, pass daily through the institutions that they founded, and traverse the very roads that they laid down long ago. But the dead speak softly to those who would listen, to those who take time to wander through their final resting places. Hundreds of graveyards pepper the landscapes of Pennsylvania's three original counties. Some are bordered by iron gates, in the old belief that this would keep restless spirits from wandering. Others are sprawled across secluded tracts of land, in back yards, or obscured behind old churches or meeting halls.

These people were like us once, individuals with hopes, fears, dreams, and struggles. Young and old, rich and poor, they have all come together in a simple, silent summation of human existence. That entire lives could be condensed to brief epitaphs, and in some cases, less than that, seems almost an affront. Still, dates, names, places, and even materials and architectural styles used in crafting monuments and mausoleums reveal a wealth of information about vanished eras. In a sense, our ancestors still reside in the very towns and cities that they built. The past is the foundation on which the present rests, and to understand the latter, we must study the former. The end of the road for some is but the beginning for others.

Birmingham-Lafayette Cemetery

A Monumental Achievement

Over the course of three centuries, what began with a modest grave-yard adjacent to the Birmingham Friends Meeting House gradually grew into a sprawling, fourteen-acre tract with tree-lined walkways, looming monu-ments, and some 7,000 interments to date. In 1842 a private enterprise led to the acquisition of additional acreage for the establishment of The New Burying Ground, a non-denominational cemetery bordering the Birming-ham Friends lot. On February 27, 1891, the property was incorporated as Birmingham-Lafayette Cemetery, a name meant to reflect the original no-menclature and pay homage to a French hero of the American Revolution.

The Battle of the Brandywine, sometimes referred to as the Battle of Birmingham, was fought on September 11, 1777. Lafayette, who was twenty, was shot in the leg during the melee. A mark is still visible in one of the meeting house walls, where the building was struck with a cannon ball. Although a defeat for Revolutionary forces, the battle demonstrated to both sides that the conflict would be a prolonged affair.

John G. Taylor, a West Chester business man who served as treasurer of the Birmingham-Lafayette Cemetery, personally financed the construc-tion of monuments to his wife, two of his ancestors who fought in the Battle of the Brandywine, and to Lafayette and General Casimir Pulaski, the Pol-ish expatriate whom Benjamin Franklin persuaded to aid the cause of Ameri-can Independence. For decades, statues of Jesus, Mary, and Lazarus greeted visitors to the cemetery, but the three immense stone compartments that housed them now stand empty, as vandalism forced the removal of the figures some fifteen years ago.

A white stone octagonal schoolhouse, with a black shingle roof and a red-shuttered window on every side, sits on the southern edge of the cem-etery, near the old Birmingham Friends Meeting House. The schoolhouse was used for meetings of the cemetery association, and within its walls Taylor's controversial renovations were hotly debated. A few feet away, towards Birmingham Lane, is a rusty old water pump. Originally, there was a vault near the meetinghouse entrance where bodies were temporarily kept during cold spells, when the ground was hard and frozen. This simple storage chamber consisted of a large hole, mounded with dirt and sur-rounded by a stone wall. The proliferation of modern excavating machines like backhoes relegated graveyard receiving vaults to obsoleteness, and it was filled in during the 1950s.

In 1894, Taylor began meticulously transcribing burial records for both Birmingham-Lafayette and the old Quaker cemetery. Little sketches of birds, trees and flowers – perhaps intended to inject some levity into an otherwise dull and dreary task – periodically appear in the margins. After Taylor's death in 1913, someone else continued the entries until 1930. The heavily bound notebook is currently kept at the Chester County Historical Society in West Chester.

The Taylor family plot occupies a rectangular spot of ground, paved over with concrete. Interred there are Taylor and his wife, their infant daughter, Taylor's sister, aunt, uncle, and parents. Under a raised stone pavilion, the marble figure of Hannah Taylor sits contemplatively, wistfully pondering the vagaries of life and death. Her chin rests delicately on one hand, while the other hand holds a bouquet of roses. The passing of Taylor's lovely young wife in 1866, a year following the loss of their daughter, affected him profoundly, as the inscription attests:

DEAR JENNIE/OFTIMES THE FLOWERS HAVE COME AND GONE/OFTIMES THE WINTER WINDS HAVE BLOWN/AND I HAVE LEARNED TO LIVE ALONE/BUT WHETHER GRAVE OR WHETHER GAY/I HIDE THY MEMORY IN MY HEART./I HOPE WE WILL ALL MEET AGAIN NEVER TO PART/GOD KNOWS BEST. JOHN G.TAYLOR. 1894.

Some of Taylor's contemporaries saw him as a bold visionary, determined to beautify and preserve a site sacred to the memory of his own family and the history of Pennsylvania. Others saw him as a bombastic tyrant, motivated by vanity and personal ambition. But regardless, he is rightfully credited with making Birmingham-Lafayette Cemetery one of Chester County's most memorable burial grounds.

Location: Birmingham Lane and Meetinghouse Roads, 1/4 mile south of Street Road (Route 926), on left, Birmingham Township, Chester County.
Portions of the map provided by Franklin Maps, King of Prussia, Pennsylvania.

8

A huge pillar atop a ziggurat, this monument to generals Lafayette and Pulaski dominates the entrance to Birmingham-Lafayette Cemetery. West Chester businessman John G. Taylor paid for its construction in 1900.

9

This touching tribute to the late Hannah Jane Taylor was erected by her husband John in 1894, and marks the Taylor family plot in Birmingham-Lafayette Cemetery.

On September 11, 1895, John G. Taylor added this granite monument to Colonel Joseph McClellan, one of his ancestors, who fought alongside Lafayette at the Battle of Brandywine 123 years earlier. The memorial garden, built in 2000, can be seen in the background. Directly across from this marker is a much larger one, dedicated to Taylor's grandfather, Colonel Isaac Taylor.

In splendid solitude sits the monument to Colonel Isaac Taylor. The ball atop the monument reads "Col. Isaac Taylor..." and the inscription underneath "served in/Gen. Anthony Wayne Brigade/Battle of Birmingham,/Sept. 11th, 1777." Near the base of the monument "Built by grandson, John G. Taylor, 1898."

The tombstone of John G. Taylor's daughter, Rebecca P. "Rebe " Taylor, bears a bas-relief of a sleeping infant, clutching a crucifix around her neck. Little Rebecca was only four months old when she died in 1865. Taylor's wife, Hannah, died the following year, at age thirty-four.

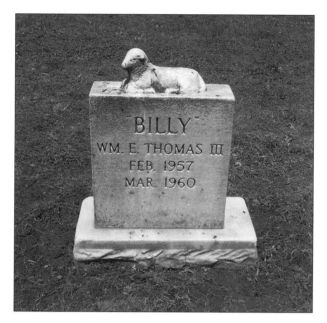

The lamb (of Christ), symbolizing innocence, appears on many tombstones of infants and small children.

Dedicated in 2000, this memorial garden is set back a few yards to the left of the main entrance to Birmingham-Lafayette Cemetery. Circular in design, the garden has four wooden benches and a granite wall at the rear where people pay to have the names of loved ones inscribed.

These huge, empty stone shelves near the entrance to Birmingham-Lafayette Cemetery once showcased statues of Jesus, Mary, and Lazarus. The figures were removed because of vandalism.

Christ Church Burial Ground

Giants in the Earth

At the corner of 5th and Arch Streets, slumbering giants rest beneath the two grassy acres of one of Philadelphia's oldest graveyards. Established in 1719 two blocks from its namesake church, this historic burial ground is the final home to many prominent citizens, instrumental in the growth of a young city and a burgeoning nation. Patriots, politicians, physicians, and lawyers lie in state among merchants, financiers, inventors, and generals. Among the esteemed interred are no less than four signers of the Declaration of Independence, the fathers of modern psychiatry and surgery, ten early mayors of Philadelphia, and the founder of the Pennsylvania Hospital. But the most famous resident of Christ Church Burial Ground is one who earned his reputation as an eighteenth-century Renaissance man – an author, publisher, diplomat, scientist, scholar, and statesman supreme – Benjamin Franklin. Franklin, who died in 1790, is buried with his wife Deborah and next to his daughter, Sarah, and son-in-law, Richard Bache. Instead of paying their respects with flowers, visitors acquired the habit of laying pennies on the large, flat stone, a tradition that endures to the present.

Prior to the advent of modern gardening techniques, sheep and other farm animals were frequently placed in graveyards to keep the grass and weeds low. Christ Church was no exception, and a wooden fence was erected in 1740 to keep the grazing animals from wandering into the city.

Encircled by a seven-foot brick wall that eventually replaced the wooden fence, Christ Church Burial Ground is almost an anachronism in the center of a bustling, vibrant city. Directly across the street are the Visitors' Center and the United States Mint, and caddy corner is the U.S. Constitution Center. On a typical weekday, the graveyard attracts a steady flow of visitors. An occasional trolley tour bus stops across the street, and announces the historic location from a loudspeaker. The ages took their toll on the old graveyard, and for over two decades, the burial ground was closed to the public. The newly refurbished cemetery opened again early in 2003, after the Old Christ Church Preservation Trust raised nearly half a million dollars for the demanding clean-up project.

The graveyard is divided into east and west sections, along either side of a dirt path that begins at the main entrance on Arch Street. Most of the stones come from blue or gray marble quarried in nearby King of Prussia.

Although less expensive than granite and easier to carve, marble is much more susceptible to erosion and acid rain. Burials in the cemetery dropped off sharply after 1840, with the last one taking place in 1997. Of the approximately 4,000 burials, maybe one-fourth have tombstones remaining. The oldest legible stone is that of Richard Wallice, who died in 1721. His marker is against the wall along Fifth Street, on the cemetery's west side. The inscription is only barely legible, and a small, hand-written marker to the right helps identify the stone.

Towards the end of the Civil War, a church official conducted a survey of existing grave markers, and assigned them Roman numerals. Along the west side of the burial ground, a red brick path lined by rows of holly trees leads to a set of iron gates, beyond which lies Fifth Street. Along either side of the path are eleven family vaults, which were built around 1810. These huge, subterranean burial chambers contain numerous decedents. Husbands, wives, children, grandchildren – and in one case, a family servant – were all buried together.

Pestilence was a common scourge in eighteenth century cities, and people compensated for the worst case scenario by having large families. Couples with ten children could expect six or seven to reach adulthood. In 1793, a brutal epidemic of Yellow Fever wiped out nearly one in ten Philadelphians, many of whom are buried in Christ Church. Extensive bloodletting was prescribed by physicians, and may well have caused more harm than good. Matthew Clarkson, who was mayor from 1792 till 1796, was revered for his firm, unwavering service to the city during one of its worst crises. Ironically, the beloved former mayor succumbed to the fever in 1800. His epitaph declares him "The heroic Matthew Clarkson."

Digging Up Dirt on the Doctor

Although he himself nearly died of Yellow Fever in 1793, physician Philip Syng Physick may have been more frightened of what might happen to him after his death. Perhaps fear of a macabre version of poetic justice prompted him to order that his grave be guarded for several weeks following his burial. Although none would have dared accuse the renowned surgeon to his face, he allegedly practiced his surgical techniques on cadavers purchased from unscrupulous gravediggers. This morbid alliance between doctors and cemetery laborers was not uncommon at the time. Nineteenth century casket manufacturers even marketed different designs meant to deter grave robbers, including a protective steel cage to enclose the casket, and a casket that was rigged to explode if moved! (Haberstein & Lamers.) One story purports that while examining a cache of stolen corpses, Physick was horrified to discover the body of his friend and mentor, Dr. Benjamin Rush. Rush, one of the signers of the Declaration of Independence, is credited with establishing modern psychiatry. During the 1793 epidemic, both he and Physick treated one another for the disease. Both men are buried near each other, in the east section.

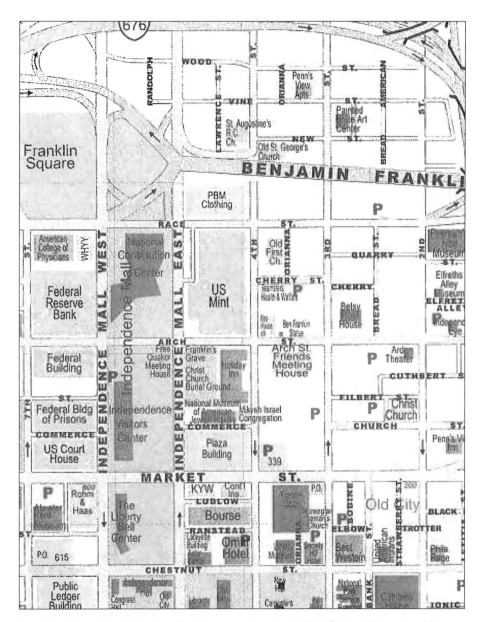

Location: 5th and Arch Streets, directly across from the United States Mint and caddy corner to the U.S. Constitution Center, Philadelphia. *Portions of the map provided by Franklin Maps, King of Prussia, Pennsylvania.*

Dozens of pennies, as well as a few nickels and dimes, cover the grave of Benjamin and Deborah Franklin. The penny-placing practice alludes to the maxim from *Poor Richard's Almanac,* "A penny saved is a penny earned." Buried next to Benjamin and Deborah Franklin are their daughter, Sarah, and their son-in-law, Richard Bache.

The oldest legible tombstone in Christ Church Burial Ground, that of Richard Wallice, who died in 1723.

The grave of Matthew Clarkson (1733-1800), fitted with a modern memorial plaque that reads: "Heroic Mayor/of Philadelphia (1792-1796)/During the 1793 Yellow Fever epidemic Matthew Clarkson died of the fever in 1800." Clarkson is one of ten Philadelphia mayors interred in Christ Church.

Facing west, towards Arch Street.

A body-snatcher? This raised stone box marks the tomb of Dr. Philip Syng Physick (1768-1837). His grandfather, noted silversmith Philip Syng (1703-1789), is buried a few feet away.

This distinctive stone, with its obelisk on top and urn in the center,
marks the grave of affluent Philadelphia businessman Tench
Francis (1731-1800) and his wife, Anne (1733-1812).

The grave of Dr. Benjamin Rush (1745-1813), the "father of modern psychiatry." Both the long, flat stone behind the modern marker and the raised box to the right are for Rush.

The grave of Peter Kurtz, Sr., longtime organist at Christ Church. This is obviously not the original marker.

Eden Cemetery

Free at Last

The epitaph on the black granite tombstone of poet and abolitionist Frances Ellen Watkins Harper (1825-1911), epitomizes the struggle and spirituality – both literally and figuratively – of many of the people interred at Eden Cemetery:

> I ASK NO MONUMENT PROUD AND HIGH
> TO ARREST THE GAZE OF PASSERS-BY
> ALL THAT MY YEARNING SPIRIT CRAVES
> IS BURY ME NOT IN A LAND OF SLAVES.

The fact that Harper was born to free parents in Baltimore, Maryland, does not lessen the impact of these lines. The official end of slavery was the beginning of a long, hard road for several generations of people, whose story mere epitaphs can barely begin to chronicle.

Established in 1902, Eden Cemetery is the oldest and largest black burial ground in the Philadelphia area. Both a consolidation of several old Philadelphia graveyards and a repository of nearly 200 years of Philadelphia's black history, Eden's fifty-three acres hold the remains of some 80,000 people. Artists, activists, entertainers, politicians, and preachers repose beneath its rolling hills and grassy fields.

In the nineteenth and early twentieth centuries, racism was as much a part of death as it was of life. Segregation was the norm in burial practices, and when sanitary concerns prompted an initiative to move cemeteries out of city limits, black graveyards were usually targeted first. Three of Eden's original four sections – Olive, Home, and Lebanon – are named for former black cemeteries, whose occupants were re-interred in Eden. Because of this mass exodus of the dead, quite a few tombstones in Eden are older than the cemetery itself. Some of the influx from condemned graveyards was handled by Mount Zion Cemetery, which is next to Eden.

The first burial in Eden came shortly after its founding, with the passing of Celestine Mosley-Cromwell, the wife of one of the cemetery's board members. Friends and family who tried to bury her were greeted by an angry mob of whites who blocked the cemetery's entrance on Springfield Road. Forced to leave to avoid a dangerous confrontation, the mourners returned to bury Cromwell the following evening. The Celestine section is named for her. Today Eden is comprised of twenty-three sections, the names honoring abolitionists, social reformers, civil rights leaders, and prominent business people, many from within Philadelphia's black community.

Also interred in the Celestine section of Eden, to the left of the entrance road that runs perpendicular to Springfield Road, is singer Marian Anderson, the contralto who overcame numerous barriers to achieve international acclaim. But even after becoming a celebrity, she frequently faced discrimination, most notably in 1939, when the Daughters of the American Revolution refused to let her perform at Washington D.C.'s Constitution Hall. First Lady Eleanor Roosevelt was so incensed that she renounced her membership in the D.A.R., and invited Anderson to give a concert at the Lincoln Memorial instead. Anderson died in 1993 at the age of ninety-six. An award in her name was established in 1998, and is given annually to artists or performers for their contributions to humanitarian causes.

A Martyr for the Cause

A lesser-known but equally important trailblazer was Octavius Valentine Catto, an early martyr for civil rights. The son of a South Carolina preacher, Catto grew up in Philadelphia, attending the Institute for Colored Youth and later teaching there. The school would eventually become Cheyney University. A political activist and role model for black youths, Catto staunchly supported both the Union cause during the Civil War and Philadelphia's Republican party, which was sympathetic to the plight of the black community. Shortly after the passage of the 15th Amendment, giving blacks the right to vote, factions within Philadelphia's Democratic party sought to disenfranchise blacks through intimidation and violence. During an election riot in the city in 1871, Catto was one of four blacks murdered at the hands of racist gangs. He was 31. In a travesty of justice not uncommon back then, his killer was tried and acquitted for both Catto's murder, and the fatal beating of another black voter. Catto was buried at Lebanon Cemetery. In 1903, his remains were exhumed and re-interred at Eden, and the section in the westernmost part of the cemetery is named for him. In a gesture perhaps long overdue, the Pennsylvania House of Representatives declared March 17 through March 23, 2003, Octavius Valentine Catto Week in Philadelphia.

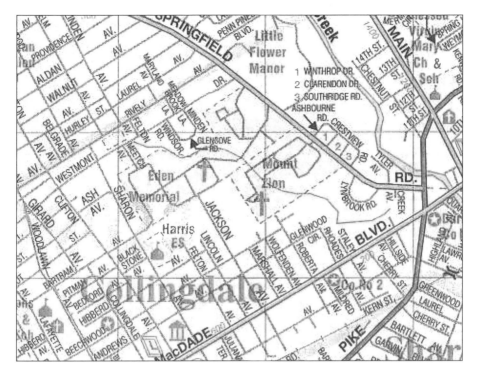

Location: Springfield Road, southeast of Westmont Drive, next to Mount Zion Cemetery, Collingdale, Delaware County. *Portions of the map provided by Franklin Maps, King of Prussia, Pennsylvania.*

The grave of opera singer Marian Anderson (1897-1993), Eden's most celebrated resident. Also buried in the family plot are her mother, Anna, and sister, Alyse. The smaller, black granite stone to the right marks the grave of Marian's brother, Richard.

This sleek, shiny tribute to the Reverend Charles Albert Tindley (1851-1933) bears a portrait of the late hymn composer, as well as the words and music to one of his most popular hymns "Beams of Heaven as I Go."

The grave of abolitionist William Still, who wrote *The Underground Railroad* in 1872.

The original tombstone for Frances Ellen Watkins Harper,
"the Bronze Muse." Also buried there is her daughter, Mary.

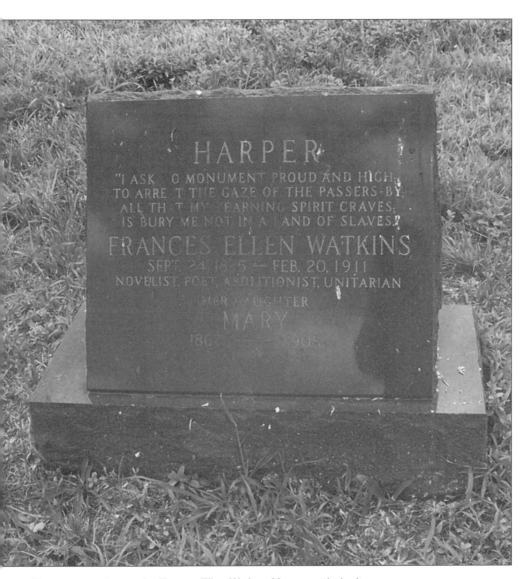

The newer tombstone for Frances Ellen Watkins Harper, with the lines from her poem "A Brighter Coming Day." Notice the discrepancy in her date of birth on the two tombstones, 1824 and 1825.

A tulip tree has grown around this tombstone in the Lebanon section of Eden Cemetery. Visible parts of the inscription read "GE WHITE/DIED/8TH 1866 AGED/RY ONLY THAT."

In the middle of the entrance drive, on a grassy median, stands a proud granite obelisk memorializing fallen black WWI soldiers.

A hillside vault in Eden Cemetery. At one time, caskets were occasionally stored inside during cold spells, but with the exception of a metal framework where the said caskets could be placed, the interior is mostly empty now. At the time of this writing, a den of foxes had found a home near the old vault, and could occasionally be seen scampering through the grass.

The only mausoleum in Eden Cemetery, that of Ethel W. (d. 1995) and Andrew J. Drew (d. 1965). The structure is only about five feet tall.

Friends Fair Hill Burial Ground

A Graveyard Resurrected

Graveyards are places frozen in time, their stone markers fading, crumbling, and gathering moss as cities spring up around them, neighborhoods slowly transform, and the surrounding landscape changes in ways that the slumbering decedents could never have imagined. Such a place is Fair Hill Burial Ground, a Quaker cemetery established in 1703 on a four-acre plot of land in what is now the Franklinville section of North Philadelphia.

A modest brick meeting house was constructed on the graveyard's southern edge, but was demolished 185 years later to make way for Cambria Street. A larger, stone building was erected around the same time, and today is occupied by Saint Mark's Outreach Baptist Church. In 1833, the graveyard was expanded to its current five-acres. At one time, a caretaker's house sat on the cemetery grounds, near the intersection of Germantown Avenue and Cambria Streets. A beautiful wrought iron fence was placed around the graveyard's perimeter in 1880, and sadly became the target of thieves and vandals a century later.

Fair Hill's darkest days came in the 1980s, after the Green Street Meeting, which owned the burial ground and meeting house, sold the property to an independent Baptist minister. Although an endowment provided a sizeable stipend to the owner for the upkeep of the historic cemetery, the property fell into decay and disarray. Sections of the old iron fence were torn off. The graveyard was strewn with litter and animal carcasses. Graffiti was spray-painted on several of the tombstones. Cultists held Satanic rituals. Worst of all, drug dealers set up shop on surrounding streets, and addicts congregated in the cemetery, tossing their used needles on the ground.

After much legal wrangling, a group of concerned Friends was able to repurchase the cemetery grounds in 1993, and the old meeting house was sold to Saint Mark's Outreach Baptist Church. Several intense cleanups were held, and dozens of volunteers as well as neighborhood residents assisted in pulling weeds, removing graffiti and picking up debris. Stolen sections of the fence were replaced with chain link. Eight years later, the burial ground was added to the National Register of Historic Places. In April of 2003, the Fair Hill Burial Ground Corporation celebrated the graveyard's 300th anniversary. Those who had assisted with the massive restoration efforts attended, as well as neighbors, politicians, and interested members of the public. Horse-drawn carriages carried fair-goers along the interior walkways, dancers performed for the crowds, and actors in costume portrayed some of the famous people buried there. Fair Hill Burial Ground Corporation holds three annual clean-up days on the second Saturday in April, July, and October. Volunteers are always welcome.

The center of the graveyard is formed by a red brick oval path, with jug handles on the northwest, northeast, and southeast respectively. Characteristic of Quaker burial grounds, the tombstones are short, simple limestone markers devoid of any epitaphs. Inscribed on the tops of the tombstones are simply the names of the deceased, and their dates of birth and death. Originally, Quakers eschewed the use of tombstones altogether. Some historians suggest that markers began appearing in Quaker cemeteries at the start of the eighteenth century, about sixty years after George Fox founded the Society of Friends. Others maintain that it was over a century later.

Some of the most prominent and outspoken social reformers of the nineteenth century are interred in Fair Hill. Men and women, these early activists espoused the dual causes of women's rights and abolition of slavery, often putting themselves in great peril. In 1838, an angry mob set fire to Philadelphia's Pennsylvania Hall because anti-slavery meetings were being held there. Four years later, rioters came close to destroying the home of Robert Purvis, a well-to-do black businessman who was both an avowed abolitionist and suffragist. Word had leaked that his house was a stop on the Underground Railroad, and that he had installed a secret room to hide runaways slaves. After the 1842 incident, Purvis and his wife Harriet moved to the more rural Byberry section of the city. Though not Quakers, both Robert and Harriet Purvis are interred in Fair Hill.

Intrepid Pioneers

The graveyard's most celebrated resident is Lucretia Mott, who combined her dedication to women's rights and the abolition of slavery by forming the Philadelphia Female Anti-Slavery Society in 1833. Most portraits of Mott depict her as a stern-looking dowager with her hair in a bun and wearing a white bonnet. Her dedication to the nascent cause of feminism was further strengthened by the rude treatment that she and other women received at the hands of the men who organized an international anti-slavery convention in London in 1840. In fact, many male abolitionists resented women's taking such an active role in the cause. Mott, an eloquent speaker and ordained Quaker minister, remained unshaken. She and four other women, including Mary Ann McClintock, helped organize the 1858 women's rights convention in Seneca Falls, New York. Although she lived to see one of the causes for which she fought so hard come to pass, Mott died nearly forty years before women were granted the right to vote. But she certainly blazed a trail for future suffragists.

Other friends and supporters of Mott who are buried in Fair Hill include Anna Jeanes, who founded Philadelphia's Jeanes Hospital and contributed substantial amounts of money to the improvement of educational opportunities for blacks. The aforementioned Mary Anne McClintock, and her husband Thomas, are also interred there, as is Edward Parrish, who in 1864 became the first president of Swarthmore College.

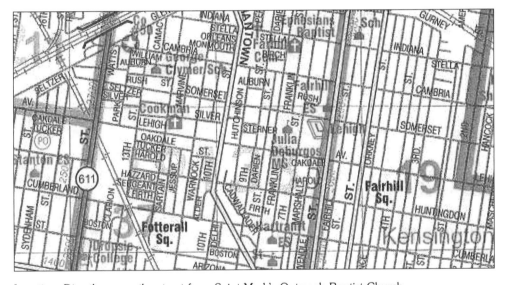

Location: Directly across the street from Saint Mark's Outreach Baptist Church (the former Fair Hill Friends Meeting House) on Cambria Street, at the intersection of Cambria Street and Germantown Avenue, Philadelphia.
Portions of the map provided by Franklin Maps, King of Prussia, Pennsylvania.

The front gates of Friends Fair Hill Burial Ground, in relatively-good condition, save for a little graffiti. In the background, at right, is a large sign with a portrait of feminist and abolitionist Lucretia Mott, and a brief history of the graveyard.

Lucretia Mott rests in the shade of a birch tree, alongside her daughter, Maria Mott Davis, and her husband, Edward M. Davis. The small, simple markers – listing only names and dates of birth and death – are paragons of Quaker simplicity.

The grave of abolitionist and businessman Robert Purvis (1810-1898).
Although both are interred in Friends Fair Hill Burial Ground, neither
Purvis nor his wife, Harriet, were Quakers.

The old Quaker meeting house on Cambria Street, across from Friends Fair Hill Burial
Ground. The building is currently occupied by Saint Mark's Outreach Baptist Church.

Gloria Dei

In the Spirit of the Swedes

The oldest tombstones in the three-acre churchyard that overlooks the western bank of the Delaware River are among the few tangible legacies of Wicaco – the tiny Swedish settlement established at the site of present-day South Philadelphia. A Native American word for "peaceful place," the meaning seems to take on particular significance for the founders and early inhabitants of the vanished hamlet, who slumber within the confines of a brick wall, shielded from the noise and traffic from adjacent Columbus Boulevard. Even the living who meander along the graveyard's dilapidated cobblestone paths find themselves somehow imbued with a sense of tranquility and wonder. Constructed in 1700, the house of worship that stands on the eastern edge of the cemetery is the oldest church building in Pennsylvania, and replaced a small wooden blockhouse used from 1677. The land for the new church was donated in September of 1697 by Sven Svenson. The original Swedish settlers who worshipped there called it Wicaco Church.

The actual congregation traces its roots to 1646, on Tinicum Island in the Delaware River. One somber reminder of the church's origins is a plaque underneath a large window on its northern wall. The inscription tells of a fountain dedicated to eight-year-old Catherine Hanson, who died October 28, 1646, and was ". . .the first white body to be laid away in the soil of the Swedish Colony which is now Pennsylvania." Catherine Hanson was buried at Tinicum Island, not in the graveyard at Columbus Boulevard and Christian Street, and there is no trace of any fountain at the latter site.

To the casual graveyard stroller, the limestone box markers prevalent in older burial grounds are often mistaken for the Egyptian-style sarcophagi, which actually contained the bodies of the deceased. But even without the benefit of modern science, eighteenth century people knew better than to simply cover a corpse with a stone lid, particularly if the dead had succumbed to one of the many virulent plagues common back then. Located near the front of the church is one such raised stone marker, its partially collapsed side clearly revealing the absence of any cadaver inside.

As with most graveyards, the older stones at Gloria Dei are in close proximity to the church. The passing of years has brought the gradual encroachment of newer markers, creeping out across the yard in all directions. Most of the newer stones are in the western section of the graveyard, in front of the church offices.

Distinguished Decedents

John C. Hunterson is buried in the northern section, a few feet from the path that runs east to west from the front of the church to the offices on Swanson Avenue. His grave is marked with a rectangular metal plaque flanked by two American flags. Under heavy fire during an engagement with Confederate forces in Virginia in 1862, the twenty-year-old private in the Third Pennsylvania Cavalry relinquished his mount to an officer whose horse had been cut down from under him, allowing the man to deliver important documents. For his actions, he was awarded the Congressional Medal of Honor in 1897 (National Park Service).

On the church's southern side is the oldest legible tombstone, that of Peter and Andreas Sandel. The stone is cracked in three separate places, and three conspicuous metal bolts attached to a plate on the back hold the marker together. Buried there are two young sons of Andreas Sandel, who was pastor from 1702 till 1719.

In life he was overshadowed by John Audubon; in death, he is literally overshadowed by holly trees. A native of Scotland, Alexander Wilson was the author of *American Ornithology*, and a contemporary of Audubon. A newer granite marker has been erected next to the original limestone box, whose inscription has completely faded. At the base of the granite stone is a quotation from the Roman poet Sextus Aurelius Propertius: "INGENIO STAT SINE MORTE DECUS" – Latin for "the honors of genius are eternal." Wilson died in 1813 of dysentery, at the age of forty-seven. Although buried at Gloria Dei, Wilson was not a parishioner.

The southwest corner of the graveyard is reserved for eight Revolutionary War officers – a brigadier general, a colonel, a major, and five captains – who could not have imagined that their mortal remains would be unceremoniously disturbed decades after their deaths. A playground on 9th Street in Philadelphia now occupies what was to be their final resting place – Ronaldson's Cemetery – and the bodies of these eight patriots, as well as the original grave markers, were relocated to Gloria Dei in 1952.

Interior Interments

A tradition dating to Medieval times, burial within the actual church building was usually reserved for high-ranking church officials. Two men are interred beneath the floor of Gloria Dei Church, both of them former pastors. The first was Swedish-born Andreas Rudman, who died in 1708. Rudman was the driving force behind the building of the church, which began in 1698. Consequently, he became the first pastor of the new church.

The second man to be entombed beneath the aisles was Nils Collin, the last Swedish pastor, who served from 1786 until his death in 1831. Sixteen years prior to his start at Gloria Dei, Collin was pastor of another church in New Jersey. During the American Revolution, he was frequently accused by the British of siding with the Revolutionaries, and vice versa. He staunchly maintained that his only allegiance was to the Swedish king, Gustaf III. Collin was a good friend of Benjamin Franklin, which may have fueled accusations by the British.

Although officially an Episcopal church since 1845, Gloria Dei is still commonly referred to as Old Swedes', in deference to the Swedish Lutherans who originally worshipped there. In 1942, the church became a National Historic Site and, in 1966, was placed on the National Register of Historic Places.

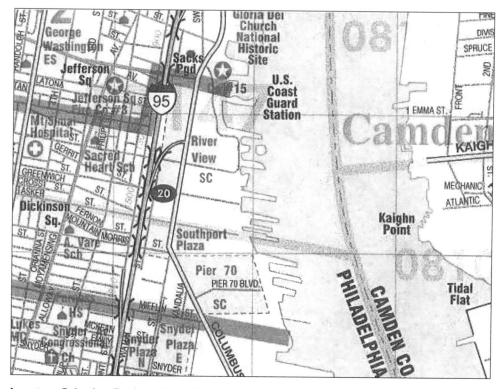

Location: Columbus Boulevard and Christian Street, west of the Delaware River, caddy corner to the Philadelphia Coast Guard Station at Columbus Boulevard and Washington Avenue. *Portions of the map provided by Franklin Maps, King of Prussia, Pennsylvania.*

The front of Gloria Dei (Old Swedes') Church, the
building's western side, which faces the graveyard.

The grave of Peter and Andreas Sandel, two infant sons of Andreas Sandel, a minister of the church. This is the oldest surviving tombstone in the cemetery.

Buried here is nineteen-year-old Lizzie Martin, who died on Christmas Eve of 1857. Because her tombstone has sunk so far down, the following epitaph is no longer visible:

"When Christmas bells rang out their chime
And holly boughs and sprigs of rhyme
Were hung on many a wall,
Our Lizzie in her beauty's prime
Lay in our darkened hall,
The Yule log burned on the hearth
We sang no song of Christmas mirth!
With hearts bowed down – with spirits riven
We gave our darling's soul to heaven." (National Park Service).

The following eight Revolutionary War officers were exhumed from the former Ronaldson's Cemetery (also known as the Philadelphia Cemetery), and re-interred at Gloria Dei: Brigadier General William Irvine, Colonel Robert Rae, Major James Moore, Captain James Peale, Captain Abraham Parsons, Captain Michael Hopkins, Captain Thomas Taylor, and Captain James F. Moore. What looks like a bush in the center of the graves is actually an ivy-covered plaque, whose inscription reads:

> PENNSYLVANIA CHAPTER/NATIONAL SOCIETY OF THE/DAUGHTERS OF
> FOUNDERS AND PATRIOTS OF AMERICA/PREPARED THIS LOT, AND/HERE
> RESET THESE TOMBSTONES/OF REVOLUTIONARY WAR OFFICERS/
> BROUGHT FROM RONALDSON'S CEMETERY, THEREBY SAVING THE SAME
> FROM DESTRUCTION/AND OBLIVION...(names of the eight officers).

The tombstone of Alexander Wilson, author of *American Ornithology*. Next to the newer granite stone is the original marker, a limestone box. The inscription on the latter has completely faded. In between Wilson's two monuments is a two and a half foot wooden stake with a numeral six, marking Wilson's grave as one of the sights in the self-guided tour pamphlet, published by the National Park Service, and available inside the church.

The grave of Peter Lamb and his wife, Isabella. The engraved anchor on the tombstone, denoting the deceased's status as a sea captain, is found on several other markers in Gloria Dei.

49

Benoni J. Pearson's epitaph bluntly defies death.

Three old tombstones rest in a corner against the church's northern wall. The inscription on the one on the left reads: "In/Memory of/WILLIAM CLARK/Son of/John and Jane Clark/ who departed this Life/on the 15th Day of July/in the Year of Our Lord/1797/Aged 4 Years and 3 Months." Colonial-era people did not take life for granted, and epitaphs frequently listed the years, months, and even days of an individual's existence (Wolf). The inscription on the middle tombstone is mostly obliterated, save for the date of 1791. The inscription on the tombstone on the right may once have read "R.I.P.", but it is unclear now.

52

A group of eighteenth century tombstones, near the southwest corner of the church. The oldest one – that of forty-two-year-old William Williamson – is front and center and dates from 1721. Five of the markers are slate, which is uncommon in Gloria Dei.

Left:
This monument, an eight-foot tall, black granite octagon with a bronze bust of John Hanson (d. 1783), the first president of the U.S. under the Articles of Confederation, was erected by the Swedish Colonial Society and the VASA Order of America in Sweden, in 1967. Other sides of the monument feature bronze emblems memorializing Johan Printz (1592-1663), listed as the first (but actually the third) governor of New Sweden; Johan Risingh (1617-1672), the last governor of New Sweden; Admiral John Dahlgren (1803-1889), who is buried at Laurel Hill; John Nystrom (1824-1885), "engineer, inventor, ship builder, author;" and John Morton (1724-1777), a signer of the Declaration of Independence. On the front of the monument is a circular bronze emblem bearing the symbol of the United States. These individuals are not buried in Gloria Dei, however.

The interior of Gloria Dei Church.

Green Mount Cemetery

Keeping Eternal Vigil

Graveyards hold many mysteries. Stone markers which sprout lopsided from the ground invite inspection, they insinuate questions to curious individuals who bend down and squint to make out their weathered inscriptions. Who were they? What did they look like? What sort of lives did they lead? And how did they meet their ends?

West Chester's Green Mount Cemetery occupies twenty-five oak-shrouded acres on the eastern edge of the borough. Established in 1861, Green Mount is the final resting place for many of West Chester's most prominent individuals – merchants, planners, politicians, and key players in the borough's early development and history.

In 1891, John G. Springer of West Chester left a substantial amount of money in his will for the construction of a 30-by-50-foot memorial chapel, to sit in what was then the center of the cemetery. With its quaint, red brick façade, sloping roof, and gray wooden porch with matching awning, the chapel complements the surrounding landscape. Services were held inside the building for a period of time, but the interior today is in a state of disrepair, the wooden pews and pulpit having long since been removed. The cemetery's board of directors hopes to eventually renovate the interior.

The Vanished Veteran

Scattered throughout the grounds of Green Mount are dozens of Civil War veterans, some who were killed in the bloody conflict, others who returned to settle and live out the rest of their lives in the area. While most of the soldiers' graves can be identified, the whereabouts of young Charley King remain unknown.

In the fall of 1861, the twelve-year-old West Chester native enlisted as a drummer boy in the Pennsylvania 49th Volunteers. One year later, his outfit came under heavy fire at the Battle of Antietam near Sharpsburg, Maryland. When the smoke had cleared after the three-day engagement, 20,000 troops lay dead, Charley among them. His father, Pennell King, wanted to return to West Chester with his son's body, but supposedly was called back into service before he was able. So Captain Benjamin Sweeney, who had taken the boy under his wing and felt somehow responsible, vowed to bring

Charley home. Some point to a slight indentation next to the grave of Charley's mother as evidence that he is interred alongside his parents. Others maintain that Charley lies in a mass grave near the site of the battle (Rodebaugh:66). A local Boy Scout troop has plans to eventually place a memorial marker for Charley next to his parents' graves.

Caretaker Dana Boyd's sentiments seem to echo those of many Chester County residents. "I hope they get something for Charley," she said. "His whole family is buried there, and his name should at least be there."

The Mystery Man in Blue and Gold

While many veterans lie at rest beneath the grassy acres of Green Mount, some are perhaps more restless. A Parkesburg woman will never forget the strange visitor that she saw on November 19, 2002. At first she thought that he was a Civil War re-enactor, or a member of one of the veterans' groups that sometimes hold memorial ceremonies in the cemetery. Reluctant at recounting her bizarre experience until her anonymity was assured, she finally began:

> He just stood there about thirty or forty feet from where I was, and he was facing the government services building (on Westtown Road), and staring straight ahead. He didn't move or say a word. He had all this Civil War stuff on him – the dark blue coat with the big gold buttons. He had a beard and long brown hair. I saw him clear as day. Then he just disappeared, literally right in front of my eyes.

Other Anonymous Anomalies

The cemetery holds other mysteries, some more macabre, like the identity of the man found dead near a Milltown farm eighty-five years ago. An article from the June 12, 1919 issue of *The Daily Local News* reads in part:

> ...The body was in such condition that a local undertaker had difficulty in handling the proposition. The face had entirely disappeared, as had other exposed portions of the body. What was left of the man was interred this forenoon at Greenmount Cemetery.

Suspicions that the body was that of a farm worker named John Gallagher later proved to be false. The deceased was buried in a pauper's grave on the northern edge of the cemetery, and the cause of death was never determined. In another anonymous grave lie the remains of a man hit by a trolley.

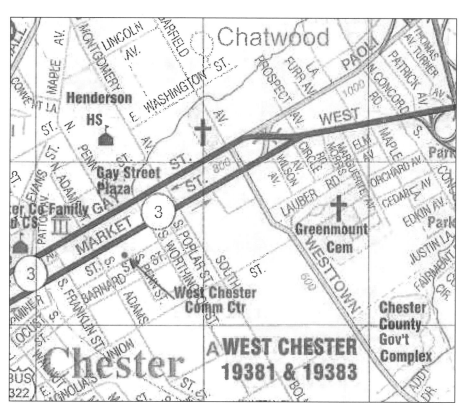

Location: 117 Westtown Road, about a 1/2 mile south of the intersection of Gay Street and Westtown Road, West Chester, Chester County. *Portions of the map provided by Franklin Maps, King of Prussia, Pennsylvania.*

The grave of Charley King's father, Pennell King. Pennell is buried next to his wife. Some point to an indentation next to Mrs. King's grave as proof that young Charley is buried alongside his parents, while others speculate that Charley's sister is buried there. Regardless of where Charley's final resting place is, there are plans to eventually erect a memorial in Green Mount Cemetery to the West Chester native, who was killed at Antietam in 1862, at the age of twelve.

Captain Benjamin Sweeney vowed to retrieve the body of
Charley King, but apparently was never able to do so.

Bayard "Bud" Sharpe, a native of West Chester. Sharpe played briefly for the Boston Braves early in the twentieth century, then went on to manage the Oakland Oaks, who won the league pennant in 1912 (Shubb).

The centerpiece of Green Mount Cemetery is the Springer Chapel. The picturesque exterior contrasts starkly to the interior, which is badly in need of renovations. The tilted square of concrete above the wooden awning reads: "MEMORIAL CHAPEL/ERECTED/ BY REQUEST OF THE LATE/JOHN G. SPRINGER/1892."

One of the ceremonial stone urns on top of the cradle marker for Mary Hoopes (1811-1879) has fallen onto the ground, at right. On the left is the tombstone of her husband, James J. Hoopes (1815-1875), and on the right, that of their daughter, Mary Ellen Keeler (1843-1867). On the back of the cradle marker is: " THIS MONUMENT/HAS BEEN ERECTED/BY DIRECTION OF/MARY HOOPES."

Laurel Hill

"I am Ozymandias..."

The concept that all are equal in death was lost on the founders of Laurel Hill, the sprawling garden cemetery established in 1836 along the eastern bank of the Schuylkill River. A bellwether in the trend to move graveyards out of the smothering confines of encroaching cities, Laurel Hill's grassy terraces, splendid sepulchral sculptures, and towering monuments clearly catered to Philadelphia's elite.

In an aggressive marketing effort, Laurel Hill's proprietors "imported" from other graveyards several Revolutionary War-era dignitaries, including Thomas McKean (1734-1817), a signer of the Declaration of Independence. These posthumous transfers did not always go smoothly, as in the case of Charles Thomson (1729-1824), Secretary to the Continental Congress. Thomson's remains were exhumed and relocated to Laurel Hill against the express wishes of his family. One story purports that two men, under cover of night, snuck into the family burial grounds at Harriton in Bryn Mawr, Pennsylvania, and began the illicit task of exhuming Thomson and his wife. In their haste to escape after nearly being spotted, they practically tossed the coffins into their wagon and fled. The bodies were later re-interred at Laurel Hill, and a monument was erected identifying them as Mr. and Mrs. Charles Thomson. Some think that the wrong people are buried there, but no one has ever bothered to check (Independence Hall Association).

During its first thirty years, Laurel Hill expanded from an original twenty acres to encompass its current ninety-five acres. A bridge constructed over Hunting Park Avenue in 1863 connected the cemetery's central and southern sections. By 1869, the mounting number of burials necessitated the purchase of 150 additional acres across the river in Lower Merion Township, thus establishing West Laurel Hill Cemetery.

The elegant Laurel Hill was as much a respite for the living as for the dead, and thousands of Philadelphians flocked there yearly to pay their respects to deceased relatives, stroll the beautifully-landscaped promenades, and picnic among the shady groves. At one point, the huge influx of visitors and tourists forced Laurel Hill's owners to begin charging admission, and restricting Sunday visitations to family members of the deceased.

The elaborate gatehouse facing Ridge Avenue marks Laurel Hill's northern entrance, and was designed by Scottish-born architect John Notman, who also drew up the plans for the cemetery's original twenty acres. Defined by an arched portal beneath an ornamental frieze and flanked by four fluted columns on either side, this inviting and imposing landmark still commands attention from passers-by. Its impressive façade has changed little in 168 years, save for the disappearance of the urn sculpture that once adorned the top. Passing across a bumpy brick path that leads through the entrance, visitors are immediately accosted by a second spectacle – a turreted stone shelter containing three statues depicting a scene from Sir Walter Scott's tale *Old Mortality*. The story's protagonist is an old Scotsman who travels the Highlands, re-engraving fading inscriptions on the tombstones of his countrymen. The scene shows Sir Walter Scott on the left, seated on a tombstone. Scott's horse stands diffidently in the background, and on the right, reclining on top of a flat grave marker, is Old Mortality himself. Atop a pedestal behind Old Mortality rests a bust of the sculptor, James Thom, minus the head.

Groves of Generals

Laurel Hill is the burial site of hundreds of Civil War veterans, among them forty generals, nearly half of whom were native Philadelphians. John Pemberton is Laurel Hill's sole Confederate general. Although born in Philadelphia in 1814, he was married to a Virginia woman, and at the outbreak of the Civil War shifted his sympathies to the South. The 1872 funeral of General George Gordon Meade, whose Army of the Potomac repulsed Robert E. Lee's assault at Gettysburg, drew hundreds of people, among them President Ulysses S. Grant. Meade is buried in the northwestern part of the cemetery, overlooking Fairmount Park and the Schuylkill River.

Death to Jefferson Davis?

The tombstone of Colonel Ulric Dahlgren, one of the youngest Union officers of the Civil War, is but a small, unobtrusive marker, reminiscent of the kind found in Quaker burial grounds. Dahlgren was killed on March 2, 1864, in Richmond, Virginia, during a raid intended to free some Union prisoners. He was twenty-one. Dahlgren had previously led successful raids against Confederate forces in Fredericksburg and Greencastle, Pennsylvania. In the summer of 1863, he lost his leg following an injury received at a battle in Hagerstown, Maryland, but was fitted with a prosthesis and returned to active duty as soon as he was able. After his death, a search of his body supposedly revealed that he and his men had orders to assassinate Confederate President Jefferson Davis and members of his cabinet. Whether this was true is subject to speculation, but nonetheless caused outrage among the Confederacy. His body was moved three or four times before finally being recovered by his father, Admiral John Dahlgren.

A Tragic Tale

Though simple compared to the dozens of obelisks shooting skyward, and the palatial mausoleums of Millionaires' Row in the cemetery's central section, the famous marble sculpture of a mother holding her two infants evokes more pathos than any other monument. A myth surrounding the statue's origins states that Helena Schaaf looks out at the spot on the Schuylkill where both of her children drowned. Actually, the first child was stillborn in 1855, and both the second child and Schaaf died during childbirth in 1857. After finishing this sad tribute to his late wife and children, a despondent Henry Dmochowksi-Saunders returned to his native Poland.

A Case of Mistaken Identity

Of all of the graveyard ghost stories, the following incident is probably the funniest. A retired Philadelphia policeman recalls a tale that he heard in the early 1960s, when he was a young sergeant with the department. Apparently, one of the officers was parked in Laurel Hill, asleep in his patrol car. Deciding to have a little fun at his expense, two of his fellow officers snuck up on their snoozing colleague. After putting a white sheet over his head, one of the miscreant cops tapped on the car window, and addressing the sleeping officer by name, said, "Come with me." Alarmed, the officer woke up, drew his gun, and fired at the mischievous "ghost." Fortunately, he missed.

Although he clearly remembers the name of the sleeping officer, the retired policeman admits that he can't vouch for the authenticity of the story.

"It was just something that I heard," he said. "There was nothing in the newspapers or anything. That would have meant an official investigation and a big hassle, so they probably just wanted to hush it up."

"The times, they are a-changing"

Although the huge crowds that visited Laurel Hill in the mid-nineteenth century have long since dissipated, the cemetery receives a fair amount of traffic. The Friends of Laurel Hill Cemetery hold several annual tours and lectures, and sponsor a Gravediggers' Ball on Mischief Night – October 30 – and a Halloween event where actors dress up as famous decedents.

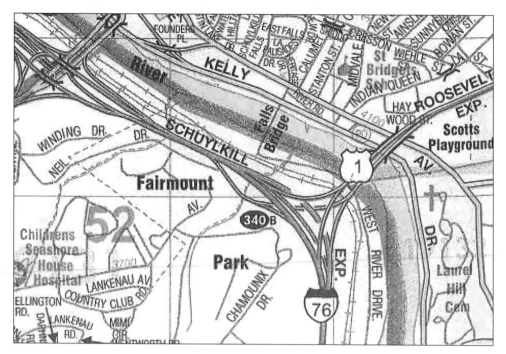

Location: Ridge Avenue, between Huntingdon Street and Allegheny Avenue, east of the
Schuylkill River, Fairmount Park and Kelly Drive. *Portions of the map provided by
Franklin Maps, King of Prussia, Pennsylvania.*

The gatehouse of Laurel Hill Cemetery, at the northern entrance, on Ridge Avenue.
This splendid façade was the concept of Scottish architect John Notman, who is
also interred in Laurel Hill. The cemetery offices are located in the gatehouse.

Atop a set of concrete steps is a group of sculptures depicting a scene from Sir Walter Scott's tale *Old Mortality*. The piece was created in the 1870s by sculptor James Thom, and purchased by Philadelphian John Jay Smith, one of Laurel Hill's founders.

Atop a rocky abutment, overlooking Kelly Drive and the Schuylkill River, is the most famous monument in Laurel Hill, one with a tragic history behind it. The white marble statue of Helena Schaaf clutches her two stillborn children. The inscription on the front reads, in part: "TO THE MEMORY/OF/HELENA SCHAFF/WIFE OF/HENRY DMOCHOWSKI-SAUNDERS..." Schaaf's husband sculpted the statue before returning to his native Poland.

The mausoleum for saw-manufacturing magnate Henry Disston and his family in Millionaires' Row. Constructed in 1878 at a cost of $60,000, Disston's mausoleum is the largest in Laurel Hill (Keels:31).

A towering obelisk marks the family plot of Edwin H. Fitler
(1825-1897), a Philadelphia businessman and former mayor.
There are many obelisks in this particular section of Laurel Hill.
According to Laurel Hill's executive director, Ross Mitchell,
obelisks started to become more popular as grave markers
around the time that the Washington Monument was built.

The monument marking the grave of General Hugh Mercer, who was originally interred at Christ Church. During a chance encounter with British forces near Trenton, New Jersey, in 1777, Mercer's contingent of American soldiers loosed an initial volley at the approaching redcoats. Before the Americans could reload, the British charged with bayonets, fatally wounding Mercer and a number of others. (Brookhiser:31).

The original tombstone for General Hugh Mercer.

Various graves in Laurel Hill Cemetery.

London Tract Cemetery

Far from the Madding Crowd

London Tract Cemetery is the quintessential country churchyard. Sitting on the western edge of the 3,200-acre White Clay Creek Preserve, the tiny graveyard and stone meeting house look much the same as they did 275 years ago, when a group of Welsh Baptists living in Delaware began the construction on land donated by parishioner John Evans. The stone wall encircling the property was added about 100 years later, as church records from 1830 make reference to payment due a Davis Whiting for its construction. Whiting died in 1860 and is buried in the graveyard. Two huge catalpa trees stand along the wall, southeast of the church's entrance. According to Park Manager Bill Morton, the trees appear in photographs of the graveyard taken a century ago, although they are smaller. Approximately 300 people are buried in London Tract. Some of the deceased are Revolutionary War veterans, whose broken, weathered stone slabs lie ingloriously atop foundations of crumbling red brick. Many graves have been ravaged by time and vandalism, their only remaining vestiges shallow depressions in the earth. Burials have mostly ceased, the exception being two cremains last year who had purchased the plots long ago, and who also had relatives interred in the graveyard.

Tick Tock?

The enduring legend of the "ticking tombstone" in London Tract Cemetery stems from an incident that supposedly occurred in 1767, during the final days of surveying for the Mason-Dixon Line. Worth noting is that the project was undertaken to resolve a land dispute between Pennsylvania and Maryland, and had nothing to do with a division between the North and the South or free versus slave states.

The first version goes that a worker on the surveying team snuck into the tent of Charles Mason and stole a pocket watch. The thief died shortly afterwards, and was somehow interred with the pilfered timepiece, which ticks inexplicably to this day. The alternate story holds that the culprit was a toddler who wandered into Mason's tent and swallowed the watch. One version names the toddler as Fithian Munuet, who grew up to become a watchmaker, of all things (Watson). When Munuet died at the age of sixty, he was buried with the watch still in his belly. But this version doesn't explain the initials "R.C." – still barely visible on the flat marble slab – and a survey done in 1999 of all the existing graves found none with the name Fithian Munuet. The ticking tombstone is located about twenty feet northeast of the church's entrance, next to the heart-shaped slate tombstone for John Devonald, who died in 1735. Devonald's stone is the oldest one in the cemetery, and the only one made of slate.

Park Manager Morton dismisses the notion that a 237-year-old chronometer still ticks beneath six feet of dirt. In fact, he has never met anyone who claims to have heard anything. What some people may have heard, Morton surmises, is the dripping caused by an underwater spring. Still, occasional ghost-hunters and curious visitors come to the graveyard, and can not resist bending down and cocking an ear. Several even maintain that they can hear something.

A Mummified Menagerie

Inside the old stone meeting house is another cemetery of sorts, but its inhabitants are not human. Mounted on the walls and lining the glass display cases on the perimeter are dozens of stuffed animals, their glazed, lifeless eyes staring at park visitors, their mouths eternally gaped in silent protest. This mummified menagerie features a variety of fish, fowl, and fauna, among them crows, turkeys, pheasants, geese, swans, herons, deer, foxes, woodchucks, and beavers. A mink, tiny fangs bared, eternally stalks its prey. Nearby, the fisher – a bigger, meaner cousin – holds a limp rodent in its jaws. Small bats in one of the display cases lie alongside deer skulls and turtle shells. Behind the podium are two large vultures, one with wings spread and beak open, as if preaching to some phantom audience in the long-empty pews. On the wall behind the podium, a raven perched on a branch is perhaps cackling "nevermore." Most of the animals are indigenous to the park area, explained Morton, and were either shot by hunters or the result of roadkill. The taxidermy exhibit opened about twelve years ago, around the time that the park acquired the additional land containing the meeting house and graveyard.

Location: Sharpless and London Tract Roads, White Clay Creek Preserve, London Britain Township, Chester County. *Portions of the map provided by Franklin Maps, King of Prussia, Pennsylvania.*

The flat grave marker next to the heart-shaped slate stone for John Devonald is the infamous "ticking tombstone." The source of the alleged ticking, as well as the identity of the deceased, remain unknown.

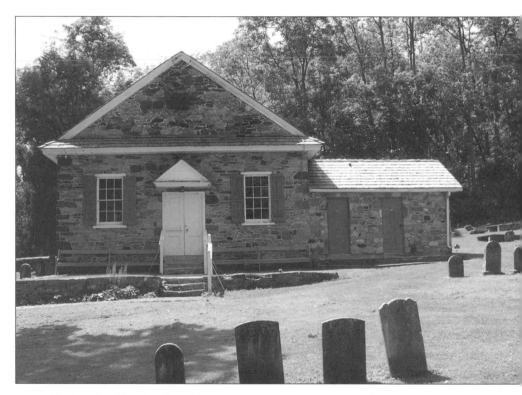

The façade of London Tract Meeting House on a sunny spring afternoon.

The interior of London Tract Meeting House is now the Natural Environmental Education Center, part of the White Clay Creek Preserve.

Behind the pulpit inside the London Tract Meeting House,
a stuffed turkey vulture delivers a silent sermon.

The graves of David and Mary Eaton. In the early nineteenth century,
David built the home that is now used as the park manager's office.

This unique metal grave marker is that of Lillie B. Russell (4/26/1882-1/26/1897). The epitaph reads simply "Our Daughter."

The mossy tombstone of Thomas Barton, "Pastor of the Old school/Baptist Church./ at Welsh Tract, London Tract, and Rock springs..." (d. 1870).

Another view of the graveyard at the London Tract Meeting. The deteriorating condition of many sections of the old wall can clearly be seen in the background.

This marker, placed behind the meeting house and outside the wall, reads:

"MINGUANN/INDIAN TOWN/WAS LOCATED HERE/THE CHIEF/
MACHALOHA OR OWHALA/AND HIS PEOPLE/OF/ THE UNAMI GROUP/
THEIR TOTEM*THE TORTISE/OF THE LENNI LENAPE OR DELAWARES/
SOLD TO/WILLIAM PENN/THE LANDS BETWEEN THE DELAWARE RIVER/
AND THE CHESAPEAKE BAY TO THE FALLS/OF SUSQUEHANNA RIVER/
OCTOBER 18, 1683/-MARKED BY/THE PENNSYLVANIA HISTORICAL
COMMISSION/AND THE CHESTER COUNTY HISTORICAL SOCIETY/1924."

Mikveh Israel Cemetery

Levy's Legacy

Aside from dealing him an emotional blow, the death of businessman Nathan Levy's infant son in 1738 left him with a dilemma. Philadelphia's tiny Jewish community was without a burial ground, and religious law mandated that the deceased be buried in land specifically established for that purpose, usually within twenty-four hours of death. Levy appealed to William Penn's son, Thomas, the proprietor of Pennsylvania. Penn arranged for Levy to purchase a small tract to be set aside for a Jewish cemetery, near the intersection of 8th and Walnut streets. Two years later, Levy acquired an additional 900 square feet two blocks south at 8th and Spruce streets, and those interred at the original location were likely exhumed and reburied.

The graveyard was expanded twice over the next fifty years, and today occupies an area of 60' x 127'. In 1752, Nathan Levy had a short brick wall erected on the north side, facing Spruce Street, because people were apparently using the tombstones for target practice. A year prior to that, Levy had posted a notice in the *Pennsylvania Gazette*, offering a reward of twenty shillings for information leading to the arrest of the so-called "sportsmen" (Elmaleh:2). According to legend, a second slight occurred in 1777, when British troops occupying Philadelphia would line up army deserters against the wall and execute them by firing squad. Twenty-five years later, a seven-foot wall of red brick was constructed and iron gates were installed at the entrance. The graveyard became a National Historic Site in 1956, and is also on the National Register of Historic Places. In addition, Mikveh Israel Cemetery is part of Philadelphia's Independence National Historical Park.

The original graveyard actually predates the synagogue building by about forty years. The synagogue, whose name means "hope of Israel," has had four different locations and five separate buildings over the course of its existence, but has been at North 4th Street since 1975. Mikveh Israel is one of the five oldest Jewish congregations in the country. Their sister synagogue, New York's Shearith Israel, was founded in 1656, and is the country's oldest.

Some of the surnames on the tombstones are Spanish or Portuguese, because a number of early Jewish settlers in America had fled Iberian colonies in South America to escape the long arm of the Inquisition. Derisively labeled "marranos" – Spanish for "pigs" – they were Jews who converted to Catholicism under threat of torture or execution. But in secret, they practiced their chosen religion.

"Here lies..."

Nathan Levy is buried in the center of the graveyard, beneath a spreading hackberry tree. The rectangular stone slab atop a foundation of bricks has cracked and buckled from age, and the 1753 inscription is difficult to make out. A prominent member of Philadelphia's fledgling Jewish community, Levy left New York in 1737 to start a trading business with his cousin, David Franks. In 1752, Levy's ship, the Myrtilla, brought the Liberty Bell over from England.

An entire row in the northwest section of the cemetery is reserved for the Gratz family. Sadly, the Gratz line has vanished, due to both intermarriage and attrition, but the family has left a powerful legacy of social and educational contributions. Simon Gratz, for whom Gratz High School in Philadelphia is named, is buried there, as is his brother, Hyman. An endowment from Hyman's will led to the founding of Gratz College in 1893. The will had stipulated that the money be used for the education of his descendants, or in the event that there were no more descendants, for the education of Jews from Congregation Mikveh Israel. Rebecca Gratz was a staunch advocate of the empowerment of women. She died in 1869 at the age of eighty-eight, leaving no heirs. Her grace, charm, and beauty touched all who knew her. The writer Washington Irving was so impressed with her that he boasted to his friend Sir Walter Scott about what an extraordinary lady she was. Based on his friend's description of Rebecca Gratz, Scott supposedly modeled the heroine of his novel *Ivanhoe* after her.

A bronze plaque placed on the tombstone of Philip Moses Russell by the Daughters of the American Revolution incorrectly lists him as a surgeon. In fact, he was a surgeon's mate. Russell received a personal commendation from George Washington for his service to the troops at Valley Forge during the winter of 1777 to 1778.

Somewhere in the Earth

Some of the most distinguished residents of Mikveh Israel Cemetery lie in unmarked graves. The only clue to the approximate location of Benjamin Nones is a small American flag posted by groundskeepers. A French Jew, Nones enlisted at the age of twenty as a private in the American army. Nones served with distinction under General Casimir Pulaski in 1777, and was commended for his bravery. He rose to the rank of major, and commanded a 400-man unit known as "the Hebrew Legion." The unit earned is nickname because many, although not the majority, of the soldiers were Jewish. On his return to civilian life, Nones faced considerable financial

strife, and was barely able to support his large family. ⸺
affiliations subjected him to an anti-Semitic diatribe in a l⸺
which he responded with equal vehemence. A devout Je⸺
several terms as *parnas*, or president, of Congregation Mik⸺

Set amid the cobblestones at the entrance to Mikveh Israe⸺
a memorial marble slab to Haym Salomon, who served as offic⸺
Robert Morris, Superintendent of Finance during the American ⸺
As a testament to his significant financial contribution to the cause⸺ independence, visitors leave coins on Salomon's memorial. After his native Poland was partitioned in 1772, Salomon fled to America, settling first in New
York. Imprisoned by the British in 1777, he was accused of spying for the
Revolutionary forces, and sentenced to hang. He escaped to Philadelphia,
and became committed to assisting his adopted country throw off the yoke
of British rule. Fluent in several languages, Salomon used his linguistic skills
and business acumen to broker securities to foreign governments, collect-
ing a small commission for each transaction. Although he amassed nearly
$400,000 by the end of his life, his fortune was in Continental currency,
which was virtually worthless due to huge debts America had incurred during the war. Salomon died a pauper in 1785, and was buried in an unmarked grave. In 1917, his great-grandson, William, placed a memorial
plaque on the cemetery's northeastern wall.

End of an Era

The last burial was Rabbi Leon Haim Elmaleh in 1972. He lies next to
his wife, Fanny Polano Elmaleh, who died in 1966. Inscribed in the lower
right corner of Fanny's marker is a memorial to their son, David, who was
lost at sea on February 2, 1943, when his ship, the USS *Dorchester*, was
torpedoed off the coast of Greenland.

Location: Spruce Street,
between 8th and 9th streets, in
the vicinity of the Pennsylvania
Hospital, Philadelphia.
*Portions of the map provided
by Franklin Maps, King of
Prussia, Pennsylvania.*

Covered with pennies, this memorial slab to Polish Jew Haym Solomon lies at the entrance to Mikveh Israel Cemetery. This does not mark the spot where the Revolutionary War financier is buried, as the exact location remains lost to history.

This memorial plaque to Haym Solomon was placed on the cemetery's northeastern wall in 1917 by his great-grandson, William.

The graves of Rebecca Gratz (1781-1869) and her sister, Rachel
Gratz (d. 10/2/1823). Rebecca was supposedly the model for
the heroine of Sir Walter Scott's novel *Ivanhoe* (1819).

The grave of Simon Gratz, for whom Philadelphia's Simon
Gratz High School, established in 1927, is named.

Beneath a hackberry tree is the grave of Nathan
Levy, founder of Mikveh Israel Cemetery.

Right:
Philip Moses Russell, surgeon's
mate to George Washington's
troops at Valley Forge during the
campaign of 1777-1778.

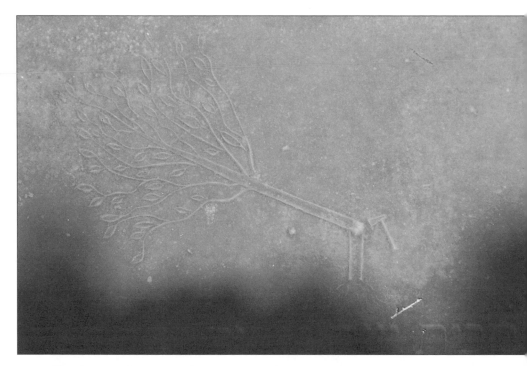

This close-up of the grave of thirteen-year-old Miriam Marks depicts a hatchet chopping down a symbolic "tree of life." The girl and her mother, forty-seven-year-old Sarah Marks, both died within two months of each other in 1784, probably of the same disease. Their graves lie side by side.

Near the entrance to Mikveh Israel Cemetery lie the shaded graves of Rabbi Leon Haim Elmaleh (d. 1972) and his wife, Fanny Polano Elmaleh (d. 1966). Rabbi Elmaleh was the last interment at the 8th and Spruce Cemetery. Three other former rabbis of Congregation Mikveh Israel are also interred in the cemetery. In the corner of Fanny's tombstone is an inscription for her son, J. David Afalo Elmaleh, who was lost at sea on February 2, 1943, on the USS *Dorchester*. His ship was torpedoed in the North Atlantic, near Greenland.

The grave of Theodor Hays (5/16/1840-12/16/1840), perhaps the youngest person buried at the 8th and Spruce Street Cemetery.

The plaque on the left pillar, outside the front gates of Mikveh Israel Cemetery: "CONSE-CRATED/1740 5500/CEMETERY/OF THE CONGREGATION MIKVE (sic) ISRAEL/ SPANISH AND PORTUGUESE/1911/E.P.S."

A shot of Mikveh Israel Cemetery, facing north.

Mount Gilead African Methodist Episcopal Church

A Balm in Gilead

Alongside a narrow, winding road that crawls lazily up a mighty slope in Bucks County, the residents of an old graveyard have finally found the peace that eluded many of them in life. The church that sits on the northern edge of this 170-year-old burial ground served as a refuge for runaway slaves, many of whom are buried in the cemetery. For them, Mount Gilead African Methodist Episcopal Church was the final stop on the Underground Railroad, and those who sought shelter in the tiny log cabin that once occupied the spot remained on Buckingham Mountain, forming a community that lived, worshipped, and died within a stone's throw of the source of their salvation. In 1852, a 32' x 52' stone church was erected on top of the original log structure, and traces of the old foundation can still be seen in the perimeter of the wooden flooring surrounding eight of the pews on the church's northern side. Ironically, the wooded hill that once sprouted clusters of small huts housing impoverished ex-slaves is now the most desirable real estate in the affluent Bucks County (Reinhardt).

A patch of tulips grows beside a rusty chain link fence that separates the graveyard from the road, and the entire place is easy to miss for those unfamiliar with the surroundings. With its white-shuttered windows and plain brick façade, the church is easily mistaken for an old schoolhouse or abandoned cottage. The tombstones are placed somewhat haphazardly – not neatly in rows or columns – with a good number congregating in the shade of a copse of dogwood trees bordering Holicong Road. Underlying bedrock posed difficulties for gravediggers, and plots shallower than six feet are marked with flat, rectangular slabs.

For a brief time in spring, a patch of white flowers from the trailing arbutus weaves its way through the grass. Much of the center of the graveyard remains unobstructed, the flat green plain only occasionally broken by a protruding stone, and the eastern side of the yard, which creeps gently downhill, provides ample room for future interments.

Marble headstones for the deceased were a luxury that many families could not afford, and the more expensive granite ones were out of the question. As a result, graves often had simple wooden crosses, or no markers at all. Because of this and incomplete records of cemetery deeds, estimating the number of people buried at Mount Gilead is difficult. Caretaker John Reinhardt guesses between 100 and 200.

Moses Hopkins, himself an escaped slave, was the first pastor of Mount Gilead, and is buried there with many of his relatives and descendants. He died in 1886, and the exact location of his grave is unknown. For a long time, his great grandson William served as caretaker, until declining health forced him to retire a few years ago. William died in June 2004, at the age of ninety-two.

"And as tall as a mountain was he"

Whether "Big Ben" is buried at Mount Gilead is unclear. Destitute and practically an invalid at the time of his death, the seven-foot-tall Benjamin Jones had escaped his slave master in Baltimore and fled to Bucks County in 1833. Well-liked by the locals, he performed odd jobs and menial chores to earn what living he could. His feet were supposedly so large that he could only afford to buy one shoe at a time, due to the cost of having each leather shoe handmade. Eleven years passed without incident, and Ben had long ago stopped looking over his shoulder. But one fateful afternoon while he was chopping firewood, he was surprised by a trio of slave hunters who had gotten wind that Ben had fled to Bucks County. Ben defended himself fiercely, but to no avail, and he was captured and returned to Maryland. The citizens of Buckingham Township rallied to his cause, raising $700 to purchase his freedom. Although Ben lived out his remaining years a free man, he was never physically the same after the severe wounds inflicted on him during the confrontation.

Evil Echoes

Like most graveyards, Mount Gilead is not without its superstitions, legends, and weird tales. Deserted for many years, the site was rumored to be a favorite haunt of Devil worshippers and bizarre cults. One tale maintains that at the stroke of midnight on a full moon, a pentagram materializes on the church door (Cassie-B).

Another legend purports that at a certain spot in front of the church, vehicles placed in neutral roll uphill, towards the graveyard, pulled by lingering forces of darkness from past Satanic rituals. In 1996, a writer for *The New York Times Magazine* described how he tested the theory, and that his car did seem to defy gravity. But he claimed that upon closer examination, he discovered that this was just an optical illusion, and that the laws of physics were not violated. The same writer also relates the "race against the Devil," in which daring teens would hop over the graveyard fence, dash across the cemetery, and touch a certain tombstone, then run back across the graveyard and leap over the fence again. If the wind blew after the runner finished, he would win a year of good luck. A gust of wind before the runner finished meant the opposite. In an alternate version, the runner had to knock on the church door first, run around the building, then jump over the fence. And the consequence of losing was almost certain death (Strong).

Caretaker Reinhardt scoffs at the ghost stories. "The only ghost here is the Holy Ghost," he says.

Although Mount Gilead has not had a regular congregation since about the 1930s, three services are held there yearly: one at Easter, one the week before Memorial Day, and one in late September or early October. During the pre-Memorial Day Service, the worshippers march out of the church while the organist plays "Battle Hymn of the Republic," and they all gather in the graveyard beneath the old oak tree on the church's western side, for a reading of the Gettysburg Address.

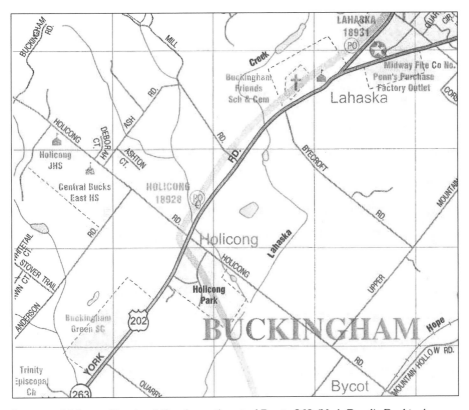

Location: Holicong Road, a 1/2 mile southeast of Route 263 (York Road), Buckingham Township, Bucks County, Pennsylvania. *Portions of the map provided by Franklin Maps, King of Prussia, Pennsylvania.*

Many relatives and descendants of ex-slave Moses Hopkins (d. 1886), Mount Gilead's first pastor, are buried in the graveyard. This tombstone is that of George Hopkins (1852-1926).

A view of Mount Gilead Cemetery, facing southeast.

Two fairly recent graves in Mount Gilead, those of Eunice A. (1909-1991) and William E. Teat (1914-2001). William played baseball in the Negro Leagues.

Buried beneath the shade of a dogwood tree on the eastern edge of the graveyard are members of the Peaker family. The diminutive marker in the foreground at left is either a footstone or the grave of a child (Reinhardt).

The tombstone of Pirmella Mitchell (1847-1893) is
slightly sunken and discolored, but still quite legible.

The Reverend Otho Scott (d. 1872).

The front of Mount Gilead A.M.E. Church, the building's
eastern side, which faces Holicong Road.

Interior of Mount Gilead A.M.E. Church, with its seven windows and eight wooden pews.

The basement and foundation of the original log cabin, which stood on the site in 1832. Now a storage room, this cramped crypt was once used for teaching Sunday School. The current resident, a black garden snake, has been seen by the caretaker on a few occasions.

Oxford Cemetery

Graveyard on the Green

About eighty years before its official incorporation in 1833, the borough of Oxford was called Hoods, after a tavern situated in the center of the small town. The first resting place for many of the original settlers in the once tiny establishment was a Presbyterian cemetery on the corner of Third and Pine streets, behind a small church building called the Sessions House. Today a huge, ancient oak holds sway on the triangular little patch of ground known as "the Green," and no trace of the old graveyard remains. The expansion of the borough led to the establishment of a new burial ground in 1855, and in 1879, the straightening of Third Street necessitated the exhuming of the bodies in the old Presbyterian Cemetery and their re-interment in the newer Oxford Cemetery. One unfortunate result of this was the loss of some of the bodies and the records of the identities of others. In 1911, road crews excavating Third Street for the installation of water pipes made a grim discovery: the displaced skeletons of several occupants of the old graveyard.

Surrounded by painted, white iron gates, this beautiful, historic cemetery occupies an entire city block, between Cemetery Road and Mount Vernon Street, on the northern edge of the borough. The wide, paved interior roads and spacious, grassy lanes provide ample room for strolling among the thousands of grave markers. The cemetery's population of roughly 10,000 is more than double that of the surrounding borough. Dozens of obelisks and protruding monuments populate the yard, juxtaposed to small, moss-covered stones, large, flat, rectangular blocks, pink granite markers, and limestone box markers. The daunting task of finding individual graves is made slightly easier by rows of alphabetical stone markers. A towering conifer and a short, spreading dogwood tree mark one of the two inner circles, where most of the older graves are. The oldest tombstone in the cemetery is that of Elizabeth Jackson, whose husband David hand-cut her simple slate marker in 1767. Hers was one of the graves moved from the old burial ground.

The first burial in the Oxford Cemetery was that of Irish-born Margaret Smith in January of 1856. David D. Dickey, one of the cemetery's founders, had the dubious distinction later that year of being the first man interred there. The prominent Dickey family was instrumental in the founding and subsequent growth of Oxford, serving as judges, politicians, merchants, and clergymen, and nearly 150 of them are buried in the cemetery. Other prominent occupants include George Washington Walton, who received the Congressional Medal of Honor for his bravery at Fort Hell, Virginia, in August of 1864, and David Jackson, who represented Pennsylvania at the 1785 Continental Congress. Hundreds of veterans, from the American Revolution to the Vietnam War, are also buried here. In 1938, a monument to unknown soldiers killed in action during World War I was erected, and later, an inscription commemorating the dead from World War II, Korea, and all future conflicts was added. Over the years, the cemetery has been a popular gathering spot for Memorial Day observances.

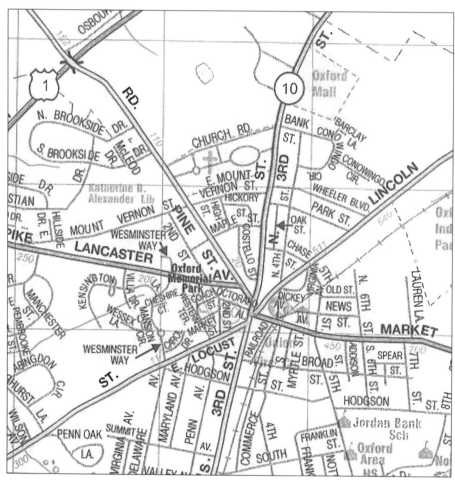

Location: Third Street (Route 10) and Cemetery Road, just past Sacred Heart Catholic Church, Oxford Borough, Chester County. *Portions of the map provided by Franklin Maps, King of Prussia, Pennsylvania.*

The oldest tombstone in Oxford Cemetery is that of Elizabeth Jackson, who died in 1767 and was originally interred in the Presbyterian cemetery on the corner of Third and Pine streets. Carved from slate by Elizabeth's husband, David, the tombstone bears the initials "EJ" on the back, and is located within the larger circle of the cemetery. The inscription on the front reads: "The memory of Elizabeth Jackson wife to David Jackson who departed this life oc (sic) the in the year of our lord 1767 Aged 34."

One of the cemetery's founders, David Dickey was the first man to be buried there, in 1856. Dozens of members of the prominent Dickey family lie in Oxford Cemetery.

Originally intended as a World War I memorial, this granite monument was placed in Oxford Cemetery in 1938. The inscription reads:

MEMORIAL/TO/WORLD WAR VETERANS/1917-1918/DEDICATED/BY/ ROY W. GIBSON POST – 535/AMERICAN LEGION/GRAY-NICHOLS POST – 1779/VETERANS FOREIGN WARS/NOVEMBER – 11 – 1938/AND IS ALSO DEDICATED TO/THE MEMORY OF/THOSE WHO GAVE THEIR LIVES/IN WORLD WAR II AND KOREA/AND THEY WHO WILL GO TO/ THEIR GREAT REWARD IN/THE WARS TO COME/A.D. 1955

This marker was placed in Oxford Cemetery on Independence Day in 1899 by members of the G.A.R. (Grand Army of the Republic), a group founded by Union veterans of the Civil War.

106

A hillside vault in Oxford Cemetery.

Some of the older tombstones in Oxford Cemetery are dark with moss and lichen.

The grave of Edna Craig Taylor, a World War I veteran.

Two unusually shaped markers flank the tombstone of Dr. William S. Thompson (1820-1870). Notice also the flat slate marker on the left.

Paoli Memorial Grounds

"Remember Paoli!"

On the cool, damp evening of September 20, 1777, 2200 American soldiers under the command of General Anthony Wayne pitched camp on a forty-acre field at the edge of a small woods. Some four miles northeast, in Tredyffrin Township, was a much larger British force led by General William Howe. Anticipating that the redcoats were planning to cross the Schuylkill River and attack Philadelphia, Wayne was anxious to make a pre-emptive strike. But he recalled the deluge that had caught both sides unprepared a week earlier at the so-called Battle of the Clouds. Hundreds of rifle cartridges had been ruined, effectively canceling the engagement. Cognizant of the impending rain this time, the general postponed his planned attack, and ordered his men to set up tents to keep the munitions dry. Tired from a long march and a harrying campaign, the Americans dropped off to sleep beneath the dark autumn skies. Many would never wake up.

Several hours later, the agonized screams of American soldiers sliced through the stillness of the camp. Men stumbled out of their crude huts to find their camp overrun with British soldiers brandishing bayonets and sabers. Without firing a shot, the British had dispatched the perimeter guards, and charged ferociously towards the slumbering Colonial forces. Bewildered Americans were skewered and slashed as they tried desperately to line up and fire a volley at their attackers. Others were impaled where they lay, or burned alive when the British set fire to their tents. In the midst of the pandemonium, the stalwart Wayne managed to round up his panicked army and escape, fleeing west. The final toll was fifty-three Americans dead, and about 150 captured or wounded. British losses numbered one or two killed, and perhaps a dozen injured.

Requiescat in Pace

The fifty-three men who perished during that nighttime ambush are buried in a common grave on the western edge of the battlefield. In 1817, a limestone obelisk was placed in the center, directly above the remains of the soldiers. On the 100th anniversary of the Paoli Massacre, a much taller granite obelisk was placed next to the original stone marker, and the barely-legible inscriptions on the older monument are replicated on the newer one. Old postcards of the graveyard show both monuments side by side. But the tremendous weight caused the granite marker to begin sinking into the ground, necessitating its relocation to a spot several yards to the south (Steinberger). Today, the huge marker occupies the most conspicuous place in the park, overlooking the twenty-three-acre memorial grounds adjacent to the battlefield. In 1964 the old wall surrounding the graveyard was rebuilt, using some of the stones from a nearby cabin that was the home of Ezekiel Bowen, who originally owned the forty-acre field. Two authentic Revolutionary War cannons flank the iron-gated entrance to the graveyard.

A grassy meadow with wooden picket fences set up along the edges, the battlefield today looks much the same as in 1777. The woods to the south are in nearly pristine condition, with the exception of a walking trail that parallels the southern edge of the battlefield. Signs posted at various locations on the battlefield detail the events of that ill-fated night.

The Second Battle of Paoli

After resting in peace for over two centuries, the dead patriots faced the threat of oblivion from developers eager to build on the hallowed ground. Another battle ensued, waged by local residents, veterans' groups, and organizations dedicated to preserving the site. In 1997, the battlefield and adjoining burial grounds were placed on the National Register of Historic Landmarks, ensuring the honored dead their well-deserved immortality. Two hundred twenty-five years to the day, a ceremony commemorating those slain at the Paoli Massacre was held, and the entire sixty-three-acre site was officially dedicated as the Paoli Memorial Grounds. Following the dedication, hundreds of actors dressed as British and Colonial soldiers re-enacted the events of that bloody September evening long ago.

Lingering Legends

The Paoli Massacre is as shrouded in legend and superstition as it is in history. One tale purports that an American soldier who lived nearby was permitted to return home and sleep in his own bed. Roused abruptly by a nightmare in which his comrades were being ruthlessly slaughtered, he jumped on his horse and raced to the Paoli encampment, despite the protestations of his wife. Arriving in the midst of the chaos, he was horrified to discover in reality what he had hoped was no more than a bad dream. Before he could recover his wits, he was decapitated by a British sword. Every September 20, the anniversary of the massacre, his ghost is said to repeat that fateful midnight ride, holding his severed head aloft like a demonic lantern (Adams).

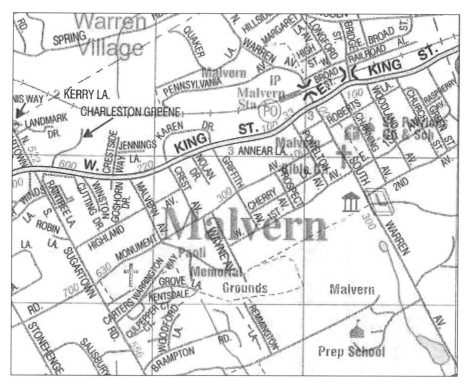

Location: Monument and Malvern Avenues (main entrance), across the street from Malvern Granite Company on the corner of Crest and Monument Avenues, Malvern, Chester County. *Portions of the map provided by Franklin Maps, King of Prussia, Pennsylvania.*

At the edge of the actual battlefield is the tiny walled cemetery where the fifty-three Americans killed during the massacre are buried. The obelisk, now encased in protective plastic, was placed there in 1817 by the Chester County Republican Artillerists. In 1964, the wall surrounding the graveyard was rebuilt with stones from a cabin once occupied by Ezekiel Bowen, who owned the field at the time of the Revolutionary War. Several American officers were quartered in Bowen's cabin during the Paoli encampment.

Left:
Erected in 1877, the 100th anniversary of the Paoli Massacre, this granite obelisk stands at the rear of the twenty-three-acre Paoli Memorial Grounds, next to the forty-acre battle-field. At one time, this massive monument stood next to the smaller one in the graveyard. The inscription on its front reads: "SACRED/TO THE MEMORY OF/THE PATRIOTS/ WHO ON THIS SPOT/FELL A SACRIFICE TO/BRITISH BARBARITY/DURING THE STRUGGLE FOR/AMERICAN INDEPENDENCE/ON THE NIGHT OF/THE 20TH SEPTEMBER 1777." Two smaller monuments in the park consist of large stones fitted with memorial plaques, and pay tribute to local men killed in action during World War II.

The Paoli battlefield, facing east.

This unusual structure, composed of old railroad tracks atop large stone blocks, seems to serve as a makeshift memorial shrine. Roughly in the center of this ten-square-foot plot of grass is a cluster of eight small American flags, surrounding three votive candles. To the right is a huge oak tree. A memorial plaque on one of the stones reads:

DEDICATED SEPTEMBER 20, 1968/BY/THE PAOLI MEMORIAL ASSOCIA-TION. THIS GRANDSTAND WAS CONSTRUCTED WITH 58 TIE BLOCKS FROM/THE TRACKS OF THE COLUMBIA AND PHILADELPHIA RAILROAD. BUILT/BY THE COMMONWEALTH OF PENNSYLVANIA IN 1834, IT WAS THE FIRST/MAJOR RAIL LINE IN AMERICA. THE BLOCKS WERE UNEARTHED IN AN/ABANDONED RAILROAD CUT IN THE NORTHWEST CORNER OF THE BOROUGH/OF MALVERN.

Plumstead Meeting Cemetery

Within and Without the Old Stone Walls

The one-acre graveyard behind Plumstead Meeting House is at its most scenic in early spring, when a rose and white blanket of tiny Mountain Pink flowers covers the ground, in colorful contrast to the stark simplicity of the fading gray tombstones. The stone for the wall surrounding this 252-year-old burial ground was taken from a small quarry located on the other side of Point Pleasant Pike, which at that time was part of the fifteen acres owned by the meeting. The site of the former quarry is now an algae-covered pond, at whose edge a large, slanting tree tilts precariously over the water.

The same year that the wall was built, the Quakers built a new meeting house with stones from the same quarry, the newer structure replacing a log cabin erected in 1730. A small sign posted on the grass a few yards north of the current meeting house marks the approximate location of the log cabin. The second meeting house was rebuilt in 1875, at which point about one-third of the meeting's property was sold to finance the project. With the exception of the fairly recent addition of a wood-burning stove, the meeting house has remained the same for over 125 years, without plumbing, heating or electricity. There is even a wooden privy with seats for two, located near the entrance.

Among the 554 marked graves in the cemetery are many of the early eighteenth-century Quakers who settled Plumstead Township. Six or seven families in particular have a large representation, among them the Browns. Thomas and Mary Brown arrived from England in 1701, settling in Philadelphia. They and their sons, Thomas, Jr. and Alexander, donated the fifteen acres that comprised the original land owned by the meeting.

Plowing a Path for Progress

Buried just inside the entrance, and several paces to the east, are Joseph and Mary Smith, who settled in Pineville, about eight miles to the southeast. An enterprising inventor as well as an industrious farmer and blacksmith, Joseph discovered a way to burn anthracite coal so that the flame produced was hot enough for forging. This he accomplished by placing the coal on a grill. Prior to that, charcoal was used primarily for forging, and producing sufficient heat was often a difficult task. Joseph also held the patent for the moldboard plow. With the conventional scratch plow, a farmer had to plow the field vertically, then crisscross it horizontally. Joseph's invention plowed the ground in both directions with a single pass, saving significant time.

The story goes that Joseph whittled the model for the moldboard plow while in the county jail in Newtown. A devout Quaker, he refused to pay the militia tax levied during the Revolutionary War, and was subsequently incarcerated (Smith).

Trying Times

Times of war were particularly difficult for Quakers. For refusing to serve in the army or contribute to the cause, they were subjected to imprisonment and seizure of their property. Those who aided either side in the conflict often faced ostracism from their fellow Quakers.

Joseph was fortunate to have the support of his friends and neighbors, and Ann, who visited her husband regularly during his imprisonment and brought him food. The Smiths eventually moved to Philadelphia, where Joseph opened a factory and amassed a considerable amount of money. He died in 1827, at the age of seventy-two. Ann died in 1854, one month short of her 100th birthday. Their great-great-great-great grandson, David, is the caretaker of the meeting house and graveyard (ibid).

In later years, Quakers softened their stance on wartime, leaving the choice of serving in the military up to each individual. In fact, several Civil War veterans are buried at Plumstead Meeting, their graves marked by small American flags. Several feet from the western side of the wall, underneath a huge ash tree, is the grave of an anonymous Civil War Veteran. Nearing the end of his life, he was destitute and without any living relatives, so he appealed to the Plumstead Friends to provide him a plot. They agreed, but because he was not a Quaker, he was relegated to burial outside the graveyard wall. The only clues to his identity are the initials "E.H." on his tombstone.

Persona Non Grata

Behind the southern wall, and at the edge of a small grove of trees, are the graves of two men who were also not welcome within the cemetery walls, but for entirely different reasons. Cousins Abraham and Levi Doan were part of a band of brigands that terrorized Bucks County for nearly a decade, during and after the American Revolution. The leaders of this gang were Joseph, his three brothers – Moses, Aaron, and Mahlon – and Abraham, a cousin. In total, the group had some thirty members. Favorite targets of the Doan gang were tax collectors and government officials, though they were not above waylaying and murdering anyone whom they thought was carrying a lot of money. Their biggest take was the robbery of the county treasury in Newtown. This was especially brazen, as the little treasury building stood in between the jail and the courthouse.

There is some speculation that the Doan gang had Tory sympathies, while others think that they simply took advantage of a chaotic situation of a country at war. Caretaker David Smith brings up a point that lends credence to the latter theory: there was a general pardon issued after the war to those who had sided with the British monarchy, but rather than avail themselves of an opportunity to "go straight," the outlaws persisted in their wicked ways. In 1783, Moses was killed in a shootout with a posse. The following year, Joseph escaped from prison and fled to Canada, where he started a family, and lived to be a very old man. Levi and Abraham were less fortunate. Both were hanged in Philadelphia in 1788. The deceased felons languished in obscurity behind the south wall for nearly two centuries, until their descendants erected markers in the 1960s. The epitaph on each tombstone makes no apologies or false professions of piety, proclaiming simply "AN OUTLAW."

Although obviously not practicing Quakers themselves, the Doans came from a prominent Quaker family in Bucks County. Their ancestor, Daniel Doan, an English convert to the Quaker faith, emigrated to America in 1696. Although the descendants of the Doans no longer live in Bucks County, they hold occasional family reunions, sometimes visiting their relatives interred at Plumstead Meeting.

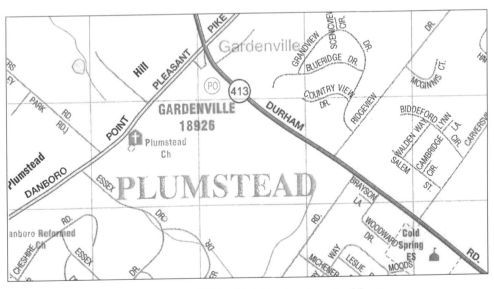

Location: Point Pleasant Pike, north of Valley Park Road and south of Route 413, Gardenville, Plumstead Township, Bucks County, Pennsylvania. *Portions of the map provided by Franklin Maps, King of Prussia, Pennsylvania.*

Stones dark with age sprout from the grassy turf in Plumstead Meeting Cemetery. Graves of veterans are indicated by an American flag and a metal marker reading G.A.R. (Grand Army of the Republic).

A view of Plumstead Meeting Cemetery, taken from outside the western wall.

The entrance to Plumstead Meeting Cemetery, along the northern wall. An eight-foot tree stump stands just outside the entrance like a steadfast sentinel of this rural necropolis.

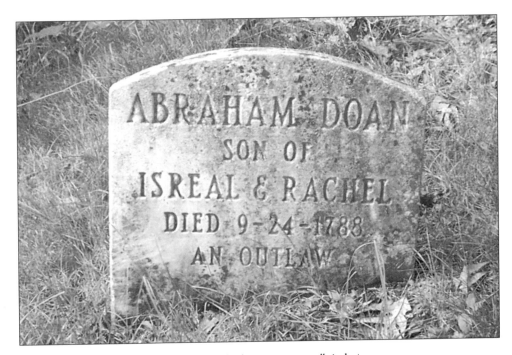

Two of the infamous Doans, buried outside the cemetery wall, in between the back (southern) wall of the cemetery and the bushes. Behind Levi's tombstone is a plain, unengraved rock, known as a native stone marker. The Doan family holds occasional reunions, and several Doans come to see interred relatives, both inside and outside of the cemetery walls.

An anonymous Civil War veteran, buried outside the
western side of the graveyard wall, under a huge ash
tree. The stone is marked "E.H."

A southern view of the Plumstead Meeting House.

Revolutionary Soldiers Cemetery

The Supreme Sacrifice

Following several initial skirmishes with enemy troops at the start of the American Revolution, the hopes of a quick victory against George III's forces were fading. The defeat suffered by the Continental Army at the Battle of Brandywine in September of 1777 took a toll on morale. The conflict was to drag on for eight years, and claim more than 25,000 American lives. The approximately 10,000 men who arrived at Valley Forge in December of 1777 under General George Washington were in for a long and difficult struggle. Soldiers were poorly equipped, food was running out, and desertion was rampant. Adequate clothing and footwear were so scarce that the dead were stripped so that the living could use their uniforms (Fulton), which must have aggravated the already unsanitary conditions. Typhoid and dysentery ravaged the encampment. By the following spring, nearly 2,000 had succumbed to disease.

The Graveyard

A tiny, walled cemetery across the street from the East Vincent United Church of Christ stands as a lasting tribute to twenty-two of those soldiers, who died from various illnesses during the spring of 1778. They were quarantined in what was then the German Reformed Church, which had been set up as a makeshift hospital for both American and British troops. The twenty-two soldiers' identities are unknown, but they symbolize the quarter million who fought for their country's independence. Each soldier has a modest steel marker that reads "Revolutionary War," capped with a small American flag. To the right of the gated entrance, amid a patch of tulips and flowering shrubs, a raised memorial plaque declares the site a historical landmark. Directly across are two other plaques commemorating the cemetery's rededication in 1997. Old Glory flies proudly from a 30-foot pole at the rear of the cemetery, behind an eight-foot limestone monument erected in 1831. The soldiers were most likely buried in a mass grave, directly underneath the monument. The inscription on the front begins: "Sacred to the memory of twenty-two Revolutionary soldiers..." Poems commemorating the fallen veterans are inscribed on either side, and on the back, the words "Virtue, Liberty and Independence."

At one time, the monument was covered by a small wooden pavilion, which has long since disappeared.

Restoring the Past

An effort spearheaded by the late Carl E. McIlroy, chairman of East Vincent Township's Historical Commission, repaired the badly-crumbling stone wall and resodded the cemetery grounds. The project took two years and cost nearly $40,000. The original wall was constructed in 1831, when the cemetery was first dedicated, and was repaired shortly after the Civil War. Heinrich Hipple, a soldier who served in the Chester County Militia in 1781, ensured that the land would be preserved for future generations.

East Vincent Supervisors, county commissioners, members of a local American Legion post, and township residents were among those who attended the July 4, 1997, rededication ceremony, to honor the anonymous interred. A TV news reporter delivered an eloquent eulogy, elaborating on the sacrifices made and the hardships endured by those who died to ensure their nation's freedom. The cemetery has long been the site of Independence Day observances.

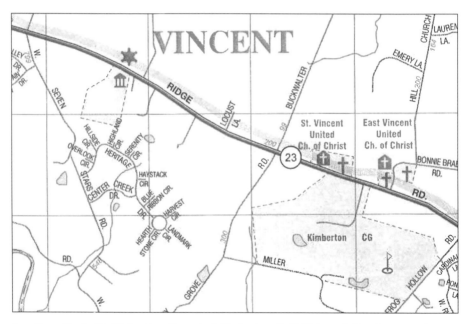

Location: Route 23 (Ridge Road), east of Kimberton Golf Club and directly across from East Vincent United Church of Christ, East Vincent Township. *Portions of the map provided by Franklin Maps, King of Prussia, Pennsylvania.*

Twenty-two steel markers capped with small American flags stand in tribute to a group of soldiers who gave their lives for the cause of independence during a brutal winter over two centuries ago. At the rear of the cemetery, Old Glory flies proudly from a thirty-foot flagpole. The limestone obelisk, with inscriptions on all four sides, was erected in 1831.

Revolutionary Soldiers Cemetery, from across Ridge Road
(Route 23), in front of East Vincent United Church of Christ.

In one corner of the cemetery, to the right of the entrance, a raised memorial plaque sprouts from a patch of tulips. The inscription reads:

Revolutionary Soldiers 1777-1778
FORGET THEM NOT
This is an historical landmark
Registered by Chester Co.
East Vincent Twp.
Penna.
        1992   C.E.M.

The initials "C.E.M." are those of former East Vincent Township Historical Commission chairman Carl E. McElroy, who oversaw the renovations.

Two memorial wall plaques inside the Revolutionary Soldiers Cemetery.
The one on the left reads:

CARL E. McILROY
A MAN WHO WOULD NOT LET
US FORGET THE MEN WHO
GAVE US LIBERTY
DEDICATED JULY 4, 2003

The one on the right reads:

Cemetery Dedicated
Nov. 19, 1831
Rededicated
July 4, 1997
East Vincent Historical
Commission

126

Saint David's Cemetery

The Wake of the Welsh

The tranquility and bucolic majesty of an early eighteenth century church and graveyard inspired poet Henry Wadsworth Longfellow in 1880 to opine:

> What an image of peace and rest
> Is this little church among its graves!
> All is so quiet, the troubled breast,
> The wounded spirit, the heart oppressed,
> Here may find the repose it craves.

The Welsh settlers who founded the congregation in 1715 had a somewhat tumultuous experience with religion. Originally Episcopalian, they became Quakers for a period of time, until they were swayed back to the Anglican Church by missionaries from the English Society for the Propagation of the Gospel in Foreign Parts. In 1789, Delaware County was established from a tract taken from the larger Chester County, and today the seven-acre graveyard at Saint David's occupies land in both counties. The oldest tombstone is that of Edward Hughes, who died December 16, 1716, at the age of fifty-six.

A Few Minor Obstacles

Renovations to the old stone church and additions to its adjacent graveyard did not always go smoothly. In 1835, plans to raze the original structure and construct a larger one on the spot were halted due to protests from Isaac Wayne, son of the late General Anthony Wayne. Some thirty-five years later, the remains of former vestryman and church warden, John Hunter, had to be moved to allow for the enlargement of the church's vestry room. Following an 1849 expansion of the graveyard, the decision to charge $10 for burial plots in the newest section irked some parishioners, as there had never been such a charge levied before. And about fifty years later, workers excavating the church floor during renovations discovered the skeletons of a man and a woman, as well as the remnants of a coffin. Church records from 1752 revealed the pair to be Alexander Bayley and his wife, Margaret. The two were subsequently re-interred in another location.

The Long-standing Reverend Currie

Buried just below the large window outside the church's eastern wall, facing Valley Forge Road, is the Reverend William Currie, who served as rector for nearly forty years. His grave is marked by a huge, flat slab, and the inscription is virtually illegible. Alongside Currie are his son, Richard, daughter-in-law, Hannah, and second wife, Lucy. In 1776, failing health and pressures from the burgeoning American Revolution prompted the sixty-three-year-old Scotsman to retire. Currie's loyalist sympathies caused him to be at odds with many parishioners, particularly when they demanded that he stop reading prayers for King George III and his family and instead substitute George Washington and members of the Continental Congress. To further complicate matters, three of Currie's six sons – Ross, William, and Richard – served in the American army. Despite Currie's continuing health problems, he lived to be 93. Over 200 years after his death, Currie still holds the record as Saint David's longest-serving rector, and his descendants are among the congregants.

Vale of the Veterans

In addition to Richard Currie, several other Revolutionary War veterans are interred at Saint David's. Sixteen anonymous casualties from the September 11, 1777, Battle of the Brandywine are rumored to be among them, though this has never been substantiated. William Burn, Jr. survived the war, but died shortly afterward in 1787. He is buried on the eastern side of the church, not far from the Curries, and about twenty feet from the wall along Valley Forge Road. His epitaph is especially poignant:

> Tho in the Paths of Death I tread
> With Gloomy Sorrow overspread
> My Steadfast Heart shall fear no Ill
> If thou, O Lord art with me still.

The haphazard and inconsistent capitalization of words in the inscription is typical of the time period. People frequently took liberties with spelling, as well, even with their own names.

Skin and Bones

Saint David's most celebrated resident is the aforementioned General Anthony Wayne, who was born in Radnor, Pennsylvania, in 1745. Wayne's fiery temper and battlefield bravado earned him the sobriquet of "Mad Anthony." He dabbled briefly in politics before and after the American Revolution, but seemed ill-suited for anything else other than a career in the military. One of George Washington's bravest and most capable generals,

Wayne campaigned tirelessly for better supplies for his men, and helped calm the waves of mutiny that erupted among several Pennsylvania regiments in 1780. His greatest triumph was the capture of the nearly impregnable British fort at Stony Point, New York, in 1779. When Washington asked the brash general if he would be willing to attack the enemy stronghold, Wayne supposedly replied, "Issue the orders, sir, and I will lay siege to Hell." Wayne's subsequent capture of the fort earned him a medal. After his death in 1796 at the age of fifty-one, Wayne was interred at Presque Isle in Erie, Pennsylvania, in accordance with his wishes. But the general's story does not end there.

Thirteen years later, Wayne's son Isaac traveled to Erie to claim his father's remains for burial in the family plot at Saint David's. When exhumed, Wayne's body was nearly completely intact, with virtually no decay. Disputes over where the general's final resting place should be led to a bizarre and gruesome compromise. Surgeon James Wallace dismembered Wayne's body, and then boiled the flesh from the bones. The skeletal remains were given to Isaac to transport back to Radnor, while the flesh was re-interred at Presque Isle. Isaac set out for the nearly 400-mile journey east, riding a horse-drawn wagon over what was later to become U.S. Route 322. The bumpy ride supposedly caused several of the general's bones to tumble out of the wagon. As a result of the ignominious treatment of his earthly remains, the general's ghost reportedly rides back and forth on a phantom steed along Route 322 every January 1st, his birthday, in search of his missing bones that were lost along the way.

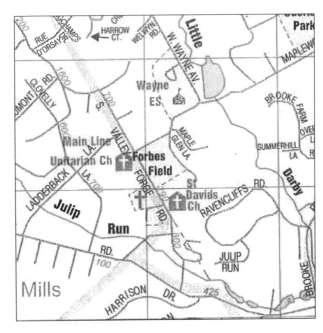

Location: Valley Forge Road, south of Radnor Township's Dittmar Park, Wayne, Pennsylvania, Chester/Delaware counties. *Portions of the map provided by Franklin Maps, King of Prussia, Pennsylvania.*

129

The grave of General "Mad Anthony" Wayne, located about 100 feet from the south side of the church, in the Wayne family plot. The stone tables in the background at right mark the graves of Wayne's son, Isaac, and Isaac's wife and children. The inscription on the front of General Wayne's obelisk reads:

> In honor of the distinguished/Military services of/MAJOR GENERAL/ANTHONY WAYNE/And as an affectionate tribute/of respect to his/memory/This stone was erected/by his companions in arms./THE PENNSYLVANIA STATE SOCIETY/OF THE CINCINNATI. July 4th A.D. 1809/Thirty fourth anniversary of/THE INDEPEN-DENCE OF THE UNITED/STATES OF AMERICA/AN EVENT/ WHICH CONSTI-TUTES/THE MOST/APPROPRIATE EULOGIAN/OF AN AMERICAN/SOLDIER AND PATRIOT.

The mostly illegible inscription on the opposite side of the monument originally read:

> Major General Anthony Wayne was born at Waynesborough, in Chester County, state of Pennsylvania, A.D. 1745. After a life of honor and usefulness he died in December, 1796, at a military post on the shores of Lake Erie, Commander-in-Chief of the Army of the United States. His military achievements are consecrated in the history of his country and in the hearts of his countrymen. His remains are here deposited (Pleasants).

Wayne's second funeral, held in 1809 after his son Isaac returned to Saint David's with (most of) his father's bones, was attended by many of the general's former comrades-in-arms, some of whom wept openly. Among those in attendance was the Welsh Reverend David Jones, who had served as a chaplain for Wayne's forces. According to one story, Jones, whose regular flock were the parishioners at Saint Peter's in Great Valley in Chester County, was a guest preacher at Saint David's during the start of the Revolutionary War, shortly following the retirement of Reverend Currie. When he noticed some young men in the front pews, he rebuked them strongly because they had not yet enlisted in the Continental Army. Jones then bellowed to the entire congregation that he himself was not afraid of the British, then peeled of his clerical vestments to reveal a Continental uniform (ibid).

Former vestryman and church warden, John Hunter, whose remains were moved circa 1870 during renovations to the church. His grave is several feet from that of General Anthony Wayne. The top of Hunter's box marker reads "TRUTH;" the base "LOVE;" the left side "CHRIST OUR HOPE;" the right side "JOHN HUNTER."

The Reverend William Currie's grave is marked by the flat stone slab underneath the large window in the church's eastern wall. Buried alongside Currie (the back row) are his son, Richard (d. 9/16/1776), daughter-in-law, Hannah, and second wife, Lucy (d. 2/14/1778). Some of Currie's parishioners only spoke Welsh, which presented obvious communication problems.

Two decrepit tombstones in Saint David's Cemetery. The one on the left is illegible. The one on the right is that of Deborah Sheaff (d. 4/6/1858, 76 years, 8 months, 20 days).

"In Memory of/WILLIAM BURN Jun./Who departed this Life/
February the 8th. 1787/Aged 30 Years..."

An angel with his head bowed sits in a patch of flowers in Saint David's Cemetery.

Saint David's Church, Wayne, Pennsylvania. Photograph taken across the street on Valley Forge Road. The inscription on the concrete slab where a window once was reads "1715." Supposedly, the church's windowpanes were destroyed during the Revolutionary War so that the lead, which supported diamond-shaped designs in the glass, could be melted down to make bullets.

One of two mausoleums in Saint David's Cemetery.

A pair of Celtic crosses in Saint David's Cemetery.

Saint James Episcopal Cemetery

From Stable to Brownstone

Some fancy lavish monuments to their memory, with prosaic epitaphs that highlight their various accomplishments and poetic verses meant to linger in the minds of the living. Others enjoy the blissful anonymity secured by the tomb, confident that future graveyard wanderers will offer no more than a cursory glance before moving on to more impressive cemetery sights. The tombstone of Thomas A. Cooper (1776-1849) makes no mention of the mounting gambling debts that caused him to flee London and settle in the quiet obscurity of a small Pennsylvania town. But neither is there any reference to his former career as a Shakespearean actor, or that his daughter married the son of U.S. President John Tyler (1841-1845).

The somewhat generic epitaph on the tombstone of Sarah Bullock has been paraphrased and replicated many times: "Who'er thou art with her here, stay read and think of me, as thou art so once was I, as I am now so thou shall be" (King:99). Bullock died on August 16, 1734, and is buried southeast of the church, near Cedar Street.

At Last, Anchored in Port

The life of Captain John Green could hardly have been sufficiently paraphrased on his tombstone, and as a result, no attempt was made to do so. A friend of John Paul Jones, his commission in the Pennsylvania State Navy in October of 1776 marked the start of long periods of separation from his wife and four children. While Alice Green apparently managed the family affairs quite capably during her husband's absences, her most difficult times came in 1779, when his ship *Nesbitt* was captured, and his entire crew imprisoned in England. Hearing rumors of the deplorable treatment of American prisoners, Alice raised as much gold as she could to secure better conditions for her husband and his men, selling most of her jewelry and cherished personal items. Later that same year, Captain Green was a free man. Undaunted by his incarceration, Green continued his seafaring adventures, sailing to the Orient six years later while in command of the merchant vessel *Empress of China* (Green & Green).

Nestled 'neath the Green Grass

Ironically, years of neglect and oblivion preserved for posterity the grave of John Henry, who is buried in the shade of a 100-foot tree several yards from the northwestern side of the church. The dust, dirt, and dead leaves that accumulated on his flat marble slab formed the perfect bed for a layer of grass, shielding his epitaph from the elements. His inscription – almost perfectly legible after 208 years – is the wordiest in the graveyard:

Here rest the Remains of/MR. JOHN HENRY/who was summoned to his Audit in a Moment/In the Twinkling of an Eye on the 16th of/October 1794 in the 48th Year of his Age/If Fortitude in every trying Situation of Life the/most exemplary Patience/under a torturing Disease/with which for more than twenty years he had been/afflicted; if singleness of Heart & Benevolence/of Disposition; the most affectionate Attention/to the Welfare & Happiness of his family & all/who looked up to Him for Assistance & Protection/join'd to a perfect Faith in Divine Revelation/can give Hope of a blissful Eternity; we may/with Confidence [illegible] from the mouldering/Mansion where his Body slumbers and seek/him in those glorious Regions where the/wicked cease from troubling and where/Tears shall be wiped from every Eye.

Henry most likely died from tuberculosis, and as a post-mortem precaution, was placed in a lead-lined coffin (Gianopoulos).

The Age of Abandonment

At the onset of the Revolutionary War, Saint James Church itself lapsed into a long period of decay and disarray. According to an 1851 sermon given by the Reverend William S. Perkins, who served as rector from 1833 to 1854, no church records exist from 1775 to 1806, and the original one-story stone structure sat dilapidated and nearly abandoned. His remarks lend credibility to the rumor that the building was used as a stable during the war:

There is now an old man, formerly a member of the vestry of this church, who recollects when this building was a mere barn, and when the cattle of this neighborhood found undisturbed shelter in it. (Anckler:39).

Sic Transit Gloria Mundi

In 1856 the old church was demolished, and the construction of a new, larger church was begun, and completed two years later. Minor renovations were done in the 1920s. Today, the brownstone, Romanesque-style building sits on the southeastern side of the churchyard, near Cedar Street, opposite the 1877 parish house. Saint James is the oldest church building in the borough of Bristol, and one of the ten oldest in the state of Pennsylvania. The mother church, Saint Mary's, sits just across the Delaware River, and her steeple can be seen from the corner of Cedar and Walnut streets. John Talbott, first pastor of Saint James (1712-1720), most likely took a rowboat from Saint Mary's in order to minister to his new Bristol congregation (Vanucci).

Grave Origins

When the first burial in Saint James occurred is not entirely clear, but correspondence from 1715 – three years before the original church was constructed – makes reference to the graveyard. The same year that construction on the new church began, the graveyard was expanded by about twenty-five yards when land was purchased from a local Baptist church. The newer portion became known as the Baptist Cemetery. A 1993 book compiling the tombstone inscriptions in Saint James lists the oldest legible one as that of Alexander DeNormandie, who died in 1724. While many Revolutionary War veterans lie in Saint James, the graveyard was also used during the conflict for temporarily storing the remains of fallen soldiers, both American and British, until their re-interment elsewhere.

Although casualties from as far back as the French and Indian Wars are buried in Saint James, the Civil War has the greatest representation. Near the rear of the church is the white obelisk that marks the grave of Captain Henry Clay Beatty, who died from wounds received at the First Battle of Manassas in 1862. Lieutenant B. Franklin Hibbs was mortally wounded that same year at Fredericksburg. The highest-ranking Union officer interred in Saint James is Brigadier General William R. Montgomery.

Dark Whispers

From the most mundane and innocuous items can grow the most sinister superstitions. When the family of Merritt P. Wright (1850-1911) placed a chair in front of his tombstone for the comfort of visitors, they would have been utterly chagrined to learn that, years later, the innocent wrought-iron piece of furniture would earn the unfortunate moniker of "the witching chair." The legend holds that those who sit in the chair at midnight during the month of October will be suddenly embraced by cold, supernatural arms. Others claim that this only occurs on Halloween. A few alleged sightings report a spectral old woman sitting in the chair. Wright's grave is behind the church, about twelve paces from the door.

The Lady of the Lake

The other ghost story associated with Saint James concerns a young woman who drowned in 1935 when she and her prom date crashed into nearby Tullytown Lake. Supposedly, her body was never recovered. Reports have surfaced intermittently about a woman in a white dress floating on the surface of the lake, or of a girl in a soaking prom dress walking along Bordertown Road. Some surmise that "Midnight Mary" is Gertrude Spring, whose tombstone is in her family plot a few yards southeast of the parish house. But the dates on her tombstone, 1909-1935, pretty much discredit that theory, as it seems unlikely that a twenty-six-year-old woman would have died on the way back from a high school prom.

Still, there are unexplained occurrences that are perhaps endemic to many old, historical sites, in particular graveyards. Father Anthony Vanucci says that he has "felt a presence" at times, though he was unsure whether it was good or bad. A former usher claimed to have seen fleeting apparitions, both in the graveyard and within the church.

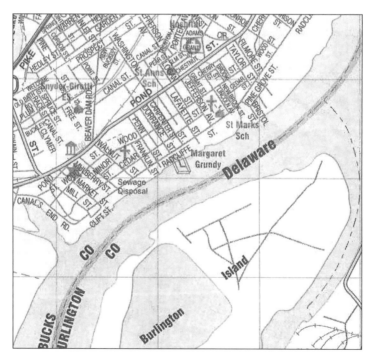

Location: Walnut Street between Wood Street and Cedar Street, Bristol borough, Bucks County. *Portions of the map provided by Franklin Maps, King of Prussia, Pennsylvania.*

The grave of Merritt P. and Sarah F. Wright, in
front of which sits the infamous "witching chair."

The only mausoleum in Saint James' graveyard is located behind the Parish house.

The front of Saint James Church and graveyard. The cradle marker at left is that of Elizabeth Boate (1818-1863); the one at right, adorned with the figure of a robed woman and a ceremonial stone urn, is that of her husband, George (1811-1858).

An elaborate double cross marker in Saint James Episcopal Cemetery.

This tombstone, with a rusty old G.A.R. POST 73 marker in front, practically leans against the southwest wall of Saint James Church. All that is legible of the inscription is ". . .in the 67th year of her age/Elizabeth Van Blonk...July 1818"

"HENRY CLAY BEATTY./Capt. [illegible] 3rd Reg. Pa. Reserves./Died September 1st 1862/of wounds received in the battle/fought on the plains of Manassas/August 30th 1862/Aged 27 years./In testimony of his worth and in/ commemoration of his service in/the cause of his country this monument/is erected by his friends fellow members/or(?) the Philadelphia Bay(?)"

Captain John (d. 1796) and Alice Green (d. 1832).

On an overcast August morning, a corpulent groundhog
sits atop a tombstone in Saint James Cemetery in Bristol.

Saint James Cemetery, facing Walnut Street. The flat stone in the foreground at left is the grave of John Henry (d. 1794).

A few yards from Saint James Parish House, in the front of the graveyard and near the fence, is a sundial marker for Robert Howard Blake (1886-1945) and Mary Stuart Dorrance Blake (1886-1971). The inscription, around four sides of the octagonal sundial, reads: "HOURS FLY/FLOWERS DIE/NEW WAYS/LOVE STAYS."

Saint Peter's Episcopal Church

Sprung from Christ Church

After nearly 250 years, the graveyard of Saint Peter's Episcopal Church at 3rd and Pine streets is nearly full, with only occasional cremation burials that are quickly using up the few remaining plots. Visitors who wander off the red brick path that winds through this Colonial-era burial ground must take care to avoid bumping into the aging tombstones that stand nearly touching one another in several sections. If one could observe a slow reversal of time, like a stop motion film being played backwards, he would notice the thousands of stone markers gradually disappear, and the rare Osage orange trees that tower amongst them shrink to mere saplings and vanish into the earth. Brick by brick, the six-foot wall surrounding the graveyard would dismantle, leaving the tombstones briefly exposed, until planks slowly filed into formation like wooden sentinels, forming a fence. Then one by one, those planks would be gone. After a few minutes, the exposed ground would once more be a grassy field, the preponderance of green broken only by the surface of a small pond. This was the scene in 1757, when William Penn's sons Richard and Thomas donated the land to build the church. The actual construction was done in 1761, to accommodate some members of Christ Church who did not want to travel as far to attend worship services. The plans were drawn up by Scottish architect Robert Smith, who also designed the steeple for Christ Church, as well as Carpenter Hall, where the first Continental Congress met in 1774. In 1832 parishioners at Saint Peter's voted to form their own congregation. In 1996, Saint Peter's Church was designated a National Historic Landmark.

Master of the High Seas

Dwarfed only by the steeple of Saint Peter's Church – which was added during the nineteenth century – the monument for naval hero Commodore Stephen Decatur (1779-1820) dominates the landscape of the graveyard. A looming, fluted column capped by an eagle with outstretched wings is the impressive tribute erected over the grave of Decatur and his wife, Susan. From the base of the stone pedestal on which the column sits to the top of the brass eagle measures about twenty feet. Decatur distinguished himself at the Battle of Tripoli in 1804, which took place during the Barbary Coast

Wars, when North African pirates in the Mediterranean where targeting American vessels. Eight years later, Decatur's ship *United States* captured the English vessel *Macedonian* during the War of 1812. Decatur was killed in a duel with a former friend, Commodore James Barron. The dispute arose over Decatur's opposition to Barron's reinstatement on the Board of Navy Commissioners, from which the latter had been suspended following a court martial several years earlier. During the 1820 confrontation in Bladensburg, Maryland, each man fired one shot, from a distance of eight feet. Decatur's bullet struck Barron in the thigh, but Barron's shot fatally injured Decatur. Decatur was originally interred in Washington, D.C., but in 1846, his remains were moved to Saint Peter's. Stephen Decatur, Sr. (1752-1808), a Revolutionary War privateer (see following), is also buried in Saint Peter's, with his wife.

Susan Wheeler Decatur died in 1860, and was originally buried at Georgetown University, because she left them a sizeable endowment in her will. When the campus expanded in 1953, they moved her to Georgetown's Holy Rood Cemetery. In 1988, she was finally interred in Saint Peter's, alongside her husband. A special ceremony was held on May 30, 1988 – Memorial Day – commemorating the event (Bernat).

Pirates and Patriots

British ships brought supplies and reinforcements to King George III's forces in the rebellious American colonies, and the Revolutionary War offered incredible opportunities to a new kind of entrepreneur – the privateer. Basically glorified pirates, these seamen purchased and equipped their own ships, and hired crews to man them. After receiving a "letter of marque" from a sovereign or government, privateers were free to attack and loot ships of enemy nations, with the understanding that they would give a portion of their plunder to the sponsoring country. Privateers had a severe impact on British shipping, capturing or destroying three times as many English ships as the Continental Navy. Gustavus Conyngham quickly became a severe nuisance to the Crown. An officer in the Continental Army, the Irish immigrant soon found a career in privateering to be much more lucrative. Setting sail from Dunkirk, France, in 1777, his ship *Surprise* quickly captured two English vessels. This enraged the English, and the French were forced to confiscate Conyngham's ship, and return the loot. Following this episode Conyngham was imprisoned briefly, but after friends secured his release, he embarked on an eighteen-month voyage of pillage and plunder. Under the auspices of the French, he captured sixty British vessels with his new ship, the fourteen-gun cutter appropriately named *Revenge* (Bobrick:383). In 1779, Conyngham was imprisoned by the British, and escaped, only to be captured again the following year. A prisoner exchange at the end of the war freed him, and the fact that he was able to keep his neck out of a British noose is remarkable. Conyngham died in 1819, and is buried at Saint Peter's under a table monument with his wife, Ann. In honor of the late Captain Conyngham, the U.S. Navy named three destroyers after him, in 1916, 1936, and 1963 (Naval Historical Center).

Hail to the (Vice) Chief

Oblivion is the first cousin of death, eventually claiming even history's most prominent men and women. The names of one-third of former U.S. Presidents are unfamiliar to most school children, and even most adults would be hard-pressed to name a handful of former Vice Presidents. Although largely forgotten by his hometown, one Philadelphia native has left an enduring legacy on a major Texas city. Born in 1792, George Mifflin Dallas had a long, distinguished political career, serving as mayor of Philadelphia, state Attorney General, Pennsylvania senator, and finally as vice president under James K. Polk, from 1845 to 1849. He died in 1864, and is entombed in a vault with eleven family members, on the east side of Saint Peter's Church, facing 3rd Street. His father, Alexander James Dallas, who was James Madison's Secretary of the Treasury from 1814 to 1816, is also buried at Saint Peter's, but not in the same vault.

Eight Little Indians

The eight (some sources say seven) Indian chiefs who came to Philadelphia in 1793 to meet with George Washington were seeking peace. The city at that time was the nation's capital, and Washington was nearing the end of his first term as President. As a young officer during the French and Indian Wars four decades earlier, Washington had been involved in several skirmishes with Native Americans, but this time, both sides met to talk rather than fight. The issue was a boundary dispute, which basically concerned the encroachment of white settlers beyond Indian lands bordered by the Ohio River, a boundary which the Indians claimed had been set forth in earlier treaties. Quoting the tribal leaders in his 1899 book *The Indian Tribes of Ohio*, Warren King Moorhead writes:

> You have talked to us about concessions. It appears strange that you should expect any from us, who have only been defending our just rights against your invasions. We want peace. Restore us to our country, and we shall be enemies no longer (33).

But while the European settlers nearly two centuries earlier brought trade, industry, and a unique culture to the shores of North America, they also brought virulent plagues, the likes of which the natives had never seen. Like so many other engagements with the white man, this one ended tragically for the Native Americans. All eight of the visiting chiefs caught a fatal dose of smallpox and were buried in unmarked graves in the cemetery's southwestern section, near 4th Street. According to Roy Bernat, a former member of Historic Saint Peter's Preservation Trust Corporation, the fact that the chiefs were buried in Saint Peter's means that they were almost certainly Christian, most likely converted by French missionaries in the Midwest. Occasionally, late night wanderers in the graveyard or people walking their dogs in the evening swear that they see phantom figures in headdresses, flitting forlornly among the graves. Other resident spooks purportedly include a spectral horse-drawn carriage and an eighteenth-century man of African descent who is fond of moonlight strolls (VisitPA). Would-be ghost hunters are advised, however, that while evening may be the best time for supernatural sightseeing, after dusk Saint Peter's graveyard is closed to the living.

Location: Pine Street, between 3rd and 4th streets, Philadelphia. *Portions of the map provided by Franklin Maps, King of Prussia, Pennsylvania.*

Painter and patriot Charles Willson Peale (1741-1827) is buried in Saint Peter's. His restored grave marker is courtesy of the Philadelphia chapter of the Daughters of the American Revolution.

The distinctive tombstone of musician and composer Benjamin Carr (1768-1831) was designed by architect William Strickland. Carr was an organist at Saint Peter's. The cost of the tombstone was paid by the Musical Fund Society, which Carr founded. The marker is in the shape of a Greek brazier, as Greek revival was popular at that time. In 1991, Carr's tombstone was vandalized, but later restored (Bernat).

John Nixon (1733-1808) was an officer during the Revolutionary War, and was instrumental in the founding of the church in 1761 (Saint Peter's Church).

The tombstone of James Roy, Esq. (d. 1836), a native of England. "Esquire" was originally a title of respect, not necessarily indicating that the person was an attorney. The broken column symbolizes a promising life cut short. The shield, Roy's family crest, reads "DEFENDENDO," which translates roughly as "Defend thyself" (Bernat).

A geometrically spectacular view of Saint Peter's graveyard, facing west, towards 4th Street.

Again facing west.

A cluster of crumbling tombstones, beneath an Osage orange tree.
In the background at right can be seen the base of the fluted
column marking the grave of Stephen and Susan Decatur.

Enclosed in an iron latticework, beneath an Osage orange tree on the church's south side, is an old, raised box marker, blackened with age and covered on its northern side with moss. The inscription is completely gone. Buried here are Hannah Moore Wilcocks (d. 9/18/1841, aged 57) and her sister, Mary Waln (d. 12/3/1841, aged 60). An 1879 compilation by assistant rector Reverend William White Bronson of all the legible tombstone inscriptions proved useful to future historians and graveyard restorers (Bernat).

Shenkel Free Burying Ground

Bones and Battle-Axes

In 1837, rumors that the graveyard next to the Second Reformed Church of Coventry was haunted might easily have been dismissed as the superstitions of simple farming folk. But the activities of a bizarre cult during the next decade, the burial in the cemetery of several cultists, and a brutal murder in an adjacent house gradually lent verisimilitude to local legends. If the place was not haunted before, some people claimed, it surely was then.

The graveyard actually predates the house of worship by over 100 years. The approximately four acres containing the church and cemetery were taken in 1784 from a 147-acre farm owned by Heinrich Shenkel, who provided for the sale of the land in his will. This officially created the Shenkel Free Burying Ground. There were interments prior to that, however, as indicated by the 1741 date on the two oldest tombstones. Because Coventry Township – prior to its eventual division into North, East, and South – had a large population of Pennsylvania Dutch, some of the tombstones in the older section have inscriptions in German. In July of 1911, the burial ground was incorporated, and the half known as the new cemetery was established.

Now That's Weird!

The followers of the cult that ran rampant through the township in the mid-nineteenth century called themselves the Battle-Axes. Their leader, Theophilus Ransom Gates, was a Connecticut-born preacher who took the name of his group from Jeremiah 51:20: "Thou art my battle-axe and weapons of war, for with thee I will destroy kingdoms." The cult's philosophy was much less austere than the Biblical passage implies. Gates openly espoused fornication and public nudity. He and several followers are reported to have marched down the aisle of the church stark naked, in flagrant defiance of the reverend, who had spoken out strongly against their practices. From a modern perspective, some of Gates's views might have been seen as progressive. He believed that women should not be forced to have babies that they did not want, he regarded monogamy as the bane of mankind, he saw no reason why businesses should be closed on Sundays, and he campaigned for the abolishment of debtors' prison. Although married,

Gates himself consorted with Hannah Williamson, who moved in with him, and who briefly assumed leadership of the Battle-Axes after his death in 1846. Six members of the Battle-Axes are buried in Shenkel Cemetery: Elizabeth, George, and Magdalene Snyder; and David, Jacob, and William Stubblebine. A few left the cult after Gates died, though, and within a short while, the Battle-Axes were only a memory.

Shades of Shingle

Several people claim to have seen the spirit of Hannah Shingle wandering the grounds of Shenkel Cemetery. In some accounts, the ghost is headless. An eccentric spinster, Hannah lived in the stone springhouse that still stands at the western edge of the graveyard. She kept a hatchet near her bed, and ironically, was murdered with her own weapon by an intruder one night. Neighbors the following morning found Hannah on the floor of her bedroom, her head literally pulverized. The culprit was never apprehended. Hannah's tombstone is located in the old section of the graveyard, on the ridge of the hill that marks the edge of the free cemetery, and shaded by a row of trees beside a green fence.

Brian C. Hardee, pastor of the Shenkel United Church of Christ, recalls driving by the cemetery one night and noticing strange, flickering lights. After pulling into the parking lot off of Shenkel Road, the intrepid clergyman went into the graveyard to investigate. Wandering among the old tombstones were three people with flashlights, looking for the ghost.

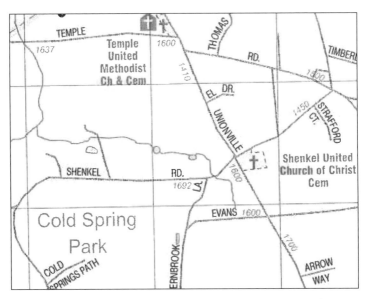

Location: Shenkel and Unionville Roads, next to Shenkel United Church of Christ, North Coventry Township, Chester County. *Portions of the map provided by Franklin Maps, King of Prussia, Pennsylvania.*

The front gates of Shenkel Cemetery, on the graveyard's northern side. The pillar at left reads:

MEMORIAL/SHENKEL FREE/BURYING GROUND/DONATED BY/HENRY SHENKEL/WILL, MAR 11, 1784/ENLARGED BY/MARY BEAR,/DEED, DEC. 25, 1858.

The pillar at right reads:

INCORPORATED/JULY 17, 1911,/COMMITTEE OF/INCORPORATION/ WILLIAM SMITH/MORGAN STUBBLEBINE/SAVILLIAN BACHMAN/ELI N. ROOT/ CHARLES YOCUM/HENRY A. KULP/ALLEN B. SMALE/FREDERICK C. FREICH/ ADDISON MAY/GEORGE BERRIKER/DANIEL KERLIN

And on the iron gates: IN MEMORY OF/JACOB S. AND MARY ROOT

Eight tombstones in the older section of the graveyard, known as the Shenkel Free Burying Ground. The red flowering bush in the background at right roughly marks the crest of the hill, where the New Cemetery begins. According to Betty Yocum, chairwoman of the North Coventry Township Historical Commission, there are still a few plots remaining in the free section.

A close-up of two of the eight stones in the Shenkel Free Burying Ground. The tombstone at right is that of I. Adams, dated 1741, one of the two oldest in the graveyard. The other 1741 tombstone, not pictured here, is that of R. Addams. The date on the tombstone at left is 1793.

The inscription on this 1807 tombstone is in German.

The older section of Shenkel Cemetery is known as the Shenkel Free Burying Ground.

The grave of Hannah Shingle, who was murdered one night in 1859 with a hatchet that she kept for protection. Whether or not she rests in peace is open to conjecture.

Slate Hill Burying Ground

Centuries of Slumber

Founded in 1690, the two-acre Slate Hill Burying Ground in Lower Makefield Township looks deceptively spacious, with wide-open patches of green between tombstones, and hardly any markers within twenty-five feet of the stone wall that runs along its western border on Yardley-Morrisville Road. But plunging a long wooden stake almost anywhere into the ground will likely disturb the bones of an eighteenth or nineteenth century Quaker, possibly even a founder of Bucks County. There is even speculation that the site was used for burials decades before being officially deeded to Falsington Friends Meeting by Thomas Janney, a Quaker minister and friend of William Penn. Originally called Slate Pit Hill, the graveyard shares the distinction with Falsington Friends Cemetery in nearby Falls Township as being the oldest burial ground in Bucks County. Both were deeded on the same day. About thirty years later, Janney's son Abel donated another acre, enlarging Slate Hill to its current size.

A Missing Methuselah

At one time, Slate Hill boasted the oldest legible tombstone in Bucks County, that of eighteen-year-old Joseph Sharp, the son of Christopher Sharp. The roughly hewn, rounded marker, dated 1698, sat slightly tilted in the center of the original one-acre tract along Yardley-Morrisville and Mahlon roads. The stone was re-cut about fifty years ago, and when the graveyard was named to the National Register of Historic Places in 1992, the inscription was fairly clear. But a visit to the site in August of 2004 by the author and a member of the Lower Makefield Historical Commission failed to find Sharp's marker. According to commission member Helen Heinz, the fact that Sharp had a tombstone as early as 1698 shows that he was probably not Quaker.

And for All the Rest

Somewhere between 1775 and 1788 – sources disagree on the exact date – Joshua Anderson donated a small tract of land, contiguous with the portion donated by Abel Janney, "for the Interment of Strangers & others"

(Stanton). This final section of the graveyard was known as the Lower Makefield Public Burying Ground, and was mainly for indigents, many of whom where farm laborers or former slaves. Although Friends were at the forefront of the abolitionist cause in the nineteenth century, some earlier Quakers owned slaves, and many had indentured servants, as well. Some Quakers voiced their opposition to slavery 100 years before Lucretia Mott's crusade, largely to no avail (Heinz).

The flowers and ferns surrounding many of the tombstones in the strangers' section lend a quaint ambience to the graves of the destitute and the forgotten, belying the hardship that characterized the lives of the deceased. Torbert Ganges served alongside his brother William in the U.S. Colored Volunteers during the final year of the Civil War. The last few years of his life were plagued with arrests and court appearances, and he died in prison in 1897, after serving one year of a six and a half-year sentence for multiple robberies. His misdeeds were well known by Lower Makefield residents. He is buried next to his brother, who died in 1901.

Samuel Harman was one of General William T. Sherman's soldiers during the infamous March to the Sea in 1865, which culminated with the burning of Colombia, South Carolina, by Union troops. Harman was described as "a colored man, 5'5", blue-eyed and blond haired," suggesting that he was of mixed parentage. While walking home one night, Harman was hit by a trolley that ran right past the graveyard, and was buried near the very spot that he was killed. Because Harman was "colored," he was not permitted to ride the trolley, and had to travel on foot (ibid). Harman's tombstone is near the northern edge of the public burying ground, a few feet from a driveway for an electrical power station.

Another black Civil War veteran, William Hill was a sailor on board the *Harvest Moon*, under the command of Admiral John Dahlgren, who is buried in Laurel Hill Cemetery. The ship struck a mine near Wilmington, North Carolina, and remains in the harbor today, under 100 feet of water (ibid). Hill survived the ship's sinking, dying in 1904 at the age of seventy-six.

The last burial in the potters' field was in 1929, when Yardley resident Gladys Frater drowned and was interred in an unmarked grave at the northernmost edge. No one has been buried in the other two sections since about 1912. Heinz estimates that there are fifty marked graves in the public burying ground, and about 200 in the rest of the graveyard. In total, about 400 people are buried at Slate Hill.

Not all of the non-Quakers in the graveyard are buried in the strangers' section. There was even an area set aside for Catholic burials around 1800, though there is no clear demarcation marking its boundaries.

Maintaining their Memory

From the early 1950s, Slate Hill was maintained by a Yardley attorney who was a member of the Falsington Friends Meeting. Around 1975, his efforts were joined by Boy Scouts and members of a local garden club. Today the graveyard is maintained by Lower Makefield Township, with assistance from the historical commission. The stone wall – which surrounds the graveyard on the north, south, and west – was rebuilt about six years ago with grant money obtained by commission members. Originally, the site was enclosed by a wooden fence.

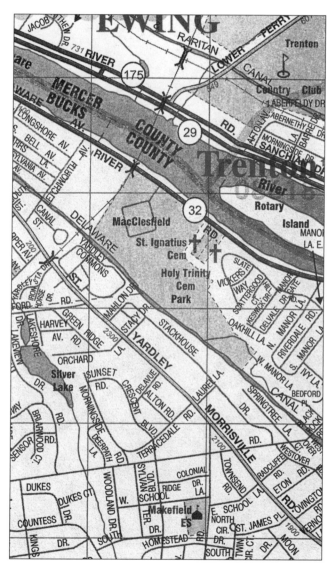

Location: Yardley-Morrisville Road and Mahlon Street, next to the Yardley Commons Apartments on Mahlon Road and a small electrical power station on Yardley-Morrisville Road, Lower Makefield Township, Bucks County. *Portions of the map provided by Franklin Maps, King of Prussia, Pennsylvania.*

A sign posted along Yardley-Morrisville Road in Lower Makefield Township marks the location of Slate Hill Burying Ground, one of the two oldest graveyards in Bucks County.

The Lower Makefield Public Burying Ground, the third section of Slate Hill, was established between 1775 and 1788 by Joshua Anderson "for the Interment of Strangers & others." Anderson and his family are buried at Slate Hill, but not in the public burying ground.

Samuel Harman, struck by a trolley while walking by the graveyard one evening, lies buried in the strangers' section of Slate Hill. After his death, Harman's widow applied for his military pension and right of burial (Heinz). A metal G.A.R. marker identifies him as a Civil War veteran.

Jefferson Mosley (d. October 1, 1908) served in Company E of the 25th Regiment of the U.S. Colored Troops during the Civil War.

The tombstone for Civil War naval veteran William H. Hill faces east, the opposite direction of most of the other markers in Slate Hill.

"IN/Memory of/Cormack Nickleson/who departed this/life Dec. 13th in the/year of Our Lord 1831." Originally, this Irish immigrant was named "McNickleson" (White).

The tombstone at left, in the southeastern section of Slate Hill Burying Ground, reads: "JONATHAN JOHNSON/Born/Oct. 23 1809/Died Aug. 15 1885/Have mercy on me O God/[illegible] to thy loving kindness." At right, behind a patch of flowers, is the headstone for Jane Johnson. Unlike most cemeteries, the footstones in Slate Hill are located behind the headstones, as in this case. But most of the graves have only a single marker, if any.

The sleek granite tombstones of brothers Alexander (d. 1883) and William Duncan
(d. 1887) stick out like proverbial sore thumbs in Slate Hill Burying Ground.
William's inscription identifies him as a Civil War veteran (Company K of the 35th
Regiment New Jersey Volunteers). The name "H. M. Swayze," in the lower right
corner of each tombstone, is likely that of the engraver.

Slate Hill Burying Ground, facing northeast. The moss-covered marker in the
foreground at left may be that of Joseph Sharp, but the inscription has vanished.

Union American Methodist Episcopal Cemetery

Home to Forgotten Heroes

About one hundred yards off a road that cuts through the center of rural East Fallowfield Township lies one of Chester County's forgotten burial grounds. Strewn haphazardly throughout the densely overgrown plot of land are between fifteen and twenty grave markers, several of them broken, overturned or illegible. Among the interred are ten black Civil War veterans. Members of the United States Colored Troops (USCT) regiments formed in 1863, they saw action in some of the fiercest battles of the four-year conflict, and settled in the Coatesville area following their military service. Not all of the deceased fought in the Civil War, as the cemetery was originally affiliated with the Union Church of Africans, constructed on the site some forty years prior. Claims of some 150 interments are unsubstantiated, and the real figure is probably closer to forty-five or fifty. An 1856 county map of the area identifies the church as Derry African, after London Derry, who sold the property to the Union Society of Colored People in 1823. In 1869 the congregation was reorganized as the Hutchinson Memorial Union American Methodist Episcopal Church, and relocated to Coatesville. When a fire destroyed the original church building in the 1930s, the graveyard was plunged into decades of neglect, abandonment, and vandalism.

In 1972, the land was seized when property taxes were not paid, which would likely not have happened had the site been listed as a cemetery and placed on the tax-exempt rolls (Young). Four years later, a Lancaster County land speculator purchased the property, unaware of its historical significance. The graveyard was rediscovered during a 1982 survey conducted by the Chester County Historical Society. Not wanting to be responsible for the upkeep, the purchaser twice attempted to sell the property. The current ownership is unclear.

For the past twenty years, the graveyard has drifted in and out of obscurity, and no less than three major restoration efforts have been conducted. The same year that the survey uncovered the graves, a local Boy Scout Troop camped there during a weekend, clearing most of the excess vegetation, righting fallen tombstones, and placing American flags by veterans' graves. A similar initiative in 1989 culminated in the cemetery's rededication the following year. Finally in 2002, a West Chester youth undertook the cleanup as his Eagle Scout project, and discussed plans to list the cemetery on the National Register of Historic Places, erect an iron fence around the perimeter, and post a marker by the roadside. But as of the writing of this book in April of 2004, the Union American Methodist Episcopal Cemetery has once again succumbed to neglect. A cursory survey of the woods reveals an area covered with brush and heavy weeds, with the only conspicuous structure being a wooden tree stand used by hunters. Two 100-foot electrical towers loom in the background, in the field on the eastern edge of the woods, and much of the surrounding land is slated for residential development. The fate of this historic burial ground is tenuous, but Margaret S. Young of the Fallowfield Historical Society surmises that in a few more years, someone else will "discover" the place, thus beginning another cycle of enthusiasm and apathy.

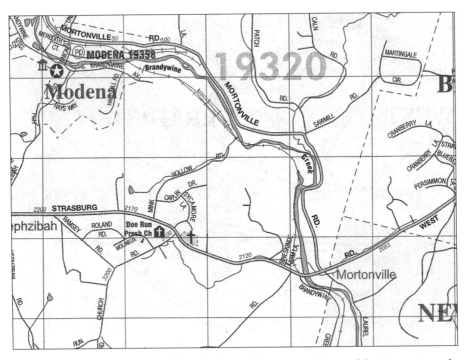

Location: Off of Caln Mortonville Road, about 200 yards southeast of the intersection of Caln Mortonville Road and Oaklyn Road, East Fallowfield Township, Chester County. *Portions of the map provided by Franklin Maps, King of Prussia, Pennsylvania.*

Another tombstone leans against the marker for George J. Brown (d. 1875). Brown is not one of the ten black Civil War veterans buried in Union American Methodist Episcopal Cemetery.

A solitary tombstone juts out amidst a backdrop of thorns, underbrush, and forest debris. A mere two years after a major clean-up effort, the old Union American Methodist Episcopal Cemetery hardly resembles a burial ground.

Susanna Dorsey (1825-1857). "In memory of Susanna, wife of
William Dorsey. Dear husband, let me sleep, I cannot dwell. Dear
Friends, do not weep, this God has made it well." (Way & Carter).

Lewis J. Henson (1840-1890) enlisted in the 6th regiment of the USCT in July of 1863 and was discharged two years later. Because a serious injury that he sustained when he was thrown from his horse in 1864 was not officially documented, Henson had difficulty applying for a pension after his military service (ibid).

John Miller's tombstone lies lopsided and partially sunken into the ground. Miller was twenty when he enlisted, and served in the same unit as Lewis J. Henson (ibid).

186

Bibliography

"13 Originals. Founding the American Colonies." *The Time Page*, 10 April 2004 <http://www.timepage.org/spl/13colony.html>.

Adams III, Charles J. *Ghost Stories of Chester County and the Brandywine Valley*. Reading, Pennsylvania: Exeter House Books, 2001.

_____. *Philadelphia Ghost Stories*. Reading, Pennsylvania: Exeter House Books, 2001.

"The American Civil War Overview. Chapter XX. The Western Theater: Sherman's March to the Sea and Campaign of the Carolinas." *Shotgun's Home of the American Civil War* (13 August 2004) <http://www.civilwarhome.com/ShermansMarch.htm>.

Augue, Karen. "Push is renewed to have graveyard tabbed as historic." *Philadelphia Inquirer* (15 March 1992).

Bacon, Allen. Telephone interview. 1 June 2004.

Beard, Adrienne. "Board acts to halt looting of old cemetery." *Philadelphia Inquirer* (12 March 1989).

Bernat, Roy. Telephone interview. 13 August 2004.

_____. Letter to the author. 20 August 2004.

Bobrick, Benson. *Angel in the Whirlwind. The Triumph of the American Revolution*. New York: Simon & Schuster, 1997.

Bolling, Deborah. "Soul Trek." *citypaper.net*. 10-16 June 2004. *The Philadelphia City Paper* (13 July 2004). <http://citypaper.net/articles/2004-06-10/cover8.shtml>.

Bower, Ronald. Telephone interview. 8 May 2004.

Boyd, Dana. Telephone interview. 28 April 2004.

Boyd, Joseph E. Personal interview. 5 May 2004.

Brookhiser, Richard. *Founding Father: Rediscovering George Washington*. New York: The Free Press, 1996.

Brooks, Michael, ed. *Laurel Hill Report*. Summer 2004. Philadelphia: The Friends of Laurel Hill Cemetery, 2004.

_____, and Anthony Waskie. *Guide To The Famous And Blameless In Laurel Hill Cemetery*. Philadelphia: The Friends of Laurel Hill Cemetery, n.d.

Burlingham, Esther, et al. *Around the Oak*. Oxford, Pennsylvania: Tricentennial Publications Committee, 1983. Reprinted by Friends of the Oxford Public Library, March 1999.

Commager, Henry Steele and Richard B. Morris, eds. *The Spirit of 'Seventy-six. The story of the American Revolution as told by participants.* New York: Harper & Row, 1958, 1967.

Cletheroe, John. "The Mason-Dixon Line." *John Cletheroe's Personal Web Site* (21 May 2004) <http://freespace.virgin.net/john.cletheroe/usa_can/usa/mas_dix.htm>.

Copley, Ann and Gaye Overdevest. *London Tract Baptist Graveyard.* Landenberg, Pennsylvania: Bureau of State Parks, 1999.

Davis, W. W. H. "The History of Bucks County, Pennsylvania, Chapter VIII, Makefield, 1692." *The History of Bucks County, Pennsylvania.* Doylestown, Pennsylvania, 1876 (13 June 2004) <http://ftp.rootsweb.com/pub/usgenweb/pa/bucks/history/local/davis/davis08.txt>.

Devlin, Anne G. "Historic Slate Hill cemetery beautified for observance." *Yardley News* (26 May 1983).

_____. "Neighborhood history gets pieced together." *Yardley News* (3 March 1983).

Doyle, Faye. Telephone interview. 14 April 2004.

Elmaleh, L. H. and J. Bunford Samuel. *The First Cemetery of Congregation Mikveh Israel,* 1906. Rev. 1962.

Fair Hill Burial Corporation. Philadelphia, 2003.

Fair Hill Burial Ground Corporation. Spring, 2003 Newsletter. Philadelphia: Fair Hill Burial Corporation.

Fair Hill Burial Ground (10 June 2004) <www.Fair Hillburial.org>.

"FAQs About Chester County." *Chester County, Pennsylvania* (16 March 2004) <http://www.chesco.org/planning/cc_faqs.html>.

Find A Grave. Jim Tipton, ed., et al. <http://www.findagrave.com>.

Forrest, Tuomi J. "William Penn. Visionary Proprietor." *American Studies at the University of Virginia.* University of Virginia (10 April 2004) <http://xroads.virginia.edu/~CAP/PENN/pnhome.html>.

"The founding of Pennsylvania." *Colonial Ancestors Database* (10 April 2004) <http://colonialancestors.com/pa/pa23.htm>.

"Frances Ellen Watkins Harper." UC Davis School of Education home page. Davis, CA. (13 July 2004) <http://education.ucdavis.edu/NEW/STC/lesson/socstud/railroad/FranBio.htm>.

Fulton, Francine. "Historic Cemetery Site Of Annual Independence Day Observance." *Community Courier.*

_____. "NSDAR Dedicates Markers At Historic Cemetery." *Community Courier.*

The General Assembly of Pennsylvania. House Resolution No. 224. 2003. (13 July 2004) <http://www2.legis.state.pa.us/WU01/LI/BI/BT/2003/0/HR0224P1437.pdf >.

Gianopoulos, Irene. "History lives at Bristol Cemetery." *Courier Times* (28 July 1992).

"Gloria Dei Church." National Park Service U.S. Dept. of the Interior home page. Washington, D.C. (21 June 2004) <http://www.nps.gov/glde>.

Gloria Dei Church. (11 July 2004) <http://www.gloriadei-oldswedes.org>.

"A Grave Matter." *Preservation* (March/April 2003): 13.

Habenstein, Robert W. and William M. Lamers. *The History of American Funeral Directing.* Milwaukee: Bullfinch Printers, Inc., 1962.

Hall, Nava. Personal interview. 28 May 2004.

HauntedPA.com. VisitPA Network, Pennsylvania Department of Community and Economic Development. (14 July 2004) <http://www.hauntedpa.com/textSite/gt14.shtml>.

Hayes, John D. "Stephen Decatur." *Encyclopedia Americana.* 2003.

"Stephen Decatur." *Dictionary of American Biography.* 1930 (1959).

Heinz, Helen. Telephone interview. 28 July 2004.

Historic Eden Cemetery Company. Collingdale, Pennsylvania: Eden Cemetery Company, n.d.

Higginbothan, Dan and Kenneth Nebenzahl. *Atlas of the American Revolution.* Chicago: Rand McNally & Company, 1974.

James, Arthur E. "Birmingham Burial Tract Opened 1721." *Daily Local News* (13 September 1962).

Jones, Randye L. "Marian Anderson (1897-1993)." *Afrocentric Voices* (15 April 2004, 13 July 2004) <http://www.afrovoices.com/anderson.html>.

Keels, Thomas H. *Philadelphia Graveyards and Cemeteries.* Charlestown, South Carolina: Arcadia Publishing, 2003.

"Laurel Hill and West Laurel Hill Cemeteries." *gophila.com.* 2003. Greater Philadelphia Tourism Marketing Corporation (6 July 2004) <http://www.gophila.com/culturefiles/sacredplaces/laurelhill>.

"Laurel Hill Cemetery At Risk." National Park Service U.S. Dept. of the Interior home page. (11 April 2000). Washington, D.C. (6 July 2004) <http://www.nps.gov/chal/sp/p01new1.htm>.

"Laurel Hill Cemetery." *ushistory.org.* 1997-2004. Independence Hall Association, Philadelphia (6 July 2004). <http://www.ushistory.org/districts/fairmountpark/laure.htm>.

Laurel Hill Cemetery. The Friends of Laurel Hill Cemetery: Philadelphia, n.d.

Leisenring, Julia B. and Patricia A.S. Forbes. *A Guide to Christ Church Philadelphia.* Philadelphia: Christ Church Preservation Trust, n.d.

"Lucretia Mott. Antislavery and Women's Rights Leader." *Lucidcafé.* Lucid Interactive,Campbell, California. (10 June 2004) <www.lucidcafe.com/library/96jan/mott.html>.

Magner, Blake A. *At Peace With Honor. The Civil War Burials of Laurel Hill Cemetery Philadelphia, Pennsylvania.* Collingswood, New Jersey: C.W. Historicals, 1997.

Map of Chester County, Pennsylvania. Alexandria,Virginia: ADC, 1997.

McNealy, Terry. Telephone interview. 2 June 2004.

_____. *Bucks County: An Illustrated History*. Doylestown, Pennsylvania: Bucks County Historical Society, 2001.

Michener, Comly. *Plumstead Friends Meeting Burial Grounds*. Doylestown, Pennsylvania: Bucks County Historical Society, April 1965.

Milgrim, Shirley. "Mikveh Israel Cemetery. The Story." *ushistory.org*. Independence Hall Association, Philadelphia (13 April 2004) <http://www.ushistory.org/mikvehisrael/index.htm>.

Moorehead, Warren King. *The Indian Tribes of Ohio*. Ohio Arch. and His. Society Publications, 1899.

Morton, William. Personal interview. 24 May 2004.

"Mount Gilead Church." *Cassie-B* (30 May 2003. 12 June 2004) <http://cassie-b.buzzstuff.net/archives/000562.html>.

Muhlenberg, Kai. *Record of interments in Shenkel Cemetery*. Eagle Scout Project, 2001. Pottstown, Pennsylvania: North Coventry Township Historical Commission.

O'Neill, Robert F. "One guest the nation has never forgotten." *Philadelphia Inquirier* (14 May 1995).

"Paoli Massacre." *ushistory.org*. Independence Hall Association, Philadelphia (6 June 2004) <http://www.ushistory.org/march/phila/paoli.htm>.

"Pennsylvania on the eve of colonization." Pennsylvania General Assembly (10 April 2004) <http://www.legis.state.pa.us/WU01/VC/visitor_info/pa_history/pa_history.htm>.

"The people of Pennyslvania." *DATING-STARTPAGE.COM* (17 March 2004) <http://www.dating-startpage.com/pennsylvania-dating-services-picture-personals.html>.

"Philadelphia County." Pennsylvania State Archives (10 April 2004) <http://www.phmc.state.pa.us/bah/dam/counties/browse.asp?catid=51>.

Pinkowski, Edward. *Chester County Place Names*. Philadelphia: Sunshine Press, 1962.

Piper, Jordan. Personal Interview. 23 June 2004.

Pleasants, Henry. *The History of Old Saint David's Church*. Philadelphia: John C. Winston Company, 1907.

"Plumstead Friends Meeting." *Bucks Quarterly Meeting of the Religious Society of Friends* (12 June 2004) <http://quakersbucks.org/plum.htm>.

Powell, Jim. "William Penn, America's First Great Champion for Liberty and Peace." *The Religious Society of Friends* (10 April 2004) <http://www.quaker.org/wmpenn.html>.

Profy, Vince. "African-Americans answered the call to arms." *Yardley News* (25 February 1993).

"A Quizzical Place." *The Philadelphia Inquirer* (13 November 2003).

Reinhardt, John. Personal Interview. 27 June 2004.

Richie, Margaret. Telephone interview. 26 May 2004.

Rodebaugh, Paul A., et al, eds. *West Chester: the First 200 Years: 1799-1999*. West Chester, Pennsylvania: West Chester Bicentennial Committee, 1999.

Saffron, Inga. "Changing Skyline. Christ Church Burial Ground to reopen for public strolling." *The Philadelphia Inquirer* (17 January 2003; 12 April 2004) <http://www.philly.com/mld/philly/living/columnists/inga_saffron/4966125.htm?1c>.

Saint David's Episcopal Church. Radnor, Pennsylvania. 2004 (16 June 2004) <http://www.stdavidschurch.org >.

Saint Peter's Episcopal Church. History and Architecture. Philadelphia, n.d.

Samuel, Bill. "William Penn." *QuakerInfo.com* (10 April 2004) <http://www.quakerinfo.com/quakpenn.shtml>.

Scheib, Clyde. Personal interview. 10 May 2004.

Sellers, Charles Coleman. *Theophilus the Battle-Axe*. 1930.

"Sextus Aurelius Propertius." Ed. John C. Shepard. *GIGA® Quote* (27 June 2004; 8 July 2004) <http://www.giga-usa.com/gigaweb1/quotes2/quautpropertiussextusax001.htm>.

Shubb, William B. "Bayard 'Bud' Sharpe." 2002. (3 May 2004) <http://oaklandoaks.tripod.com/sharpe.html>.

Smith, David. Personal interview. 18 June 2004.

Smith, James Iden et al. *Plumstead Friends Meeting. 25ᵗʰ Anniversary. August 30, 1953*. Buckingham, Pennsylvania: Buckingham Monthly Meeting of Friends, 1953.

Stanton, James E. "Cemetery named to Nat'l Register." *Courier Times* (7 July 1992).

Steinberger, Michael. Telephone interview. 5 June 2004.

Strong, Eric. "The Legend of Gravity Hill." *The New York Times Magazine* (November 1996; 13 June 2004) <http://endeavor.med.nyu.edu/~strone01/gravity.html>.

Taylor, John G., et al. *Birmingham-Lafayette Cemetery. Record of Burials*. Notebook, 1894-1930. West Chester, Pennsylvania: Chester County Historical Society.

Vanucci, Anthony. Personal interview. 1 August 2004.

Waskie, Andy. "Biography of Octavius V. Catto: 'Forgotten Black Hero of Philadelphia'." *Afrolumens Project* (13 July 2004) <http://www.afrolumens.org/rising_free/waskie1.html>.

Watson, Donna. "Ticking grave a true Halloween story." *The Coatesville Record* (30 October, 1984).

Way, Stanley H. and Lee Carter. "Remembered Civil War Soldiers." 1994. Web page of Stanley Way (15 April 2004) <http://pages.prodigy.net/stanley.way/coatesville>.

White, Florence. Personal interview. 10 August 2004.

Wilde, Robert. "The Rulers of Sweden: From 990 Until Today." *About*. New York (8 July 2004) <http://europeanhistory.about.com/library/readyref/blswedenrulers.htm>.

Williams, Kim-Eric. "Gloria Dei (Old Swedes') Church." *The Swedish Colonial Society* (1 July 2004) <http://www.colonialswedes.org/Churches/GloDei.html>.

Wittenberg, Eric J. "Biography of Ulric Dahlgren." *Buford's Boys* (6 July 2004) <http://www.bufordsboys.com/DahlgrenBio.htm>.

Wolf, Jean K. *Lives of the Silent Stones in the Christ Church Burial Ground.* Philadelphia: Christ Church Preservation Trust, 2003.

X, Jimi. "General 'Mad Anthony' Wayne." *BBC* (19 November 2001). British Broadcasting Company (16 June 2004) <http://www.bbc.co.uk/dna/h2g2/alabaster/A481682#footnote1>.

Yocum, Clara Root. *A History of Shenkel Church.* October 1972.

Young, Margaret S. Personal interview. 20 April 2003.

_____, Research notes.

Zotti, Gina. "'Patriots' observe anniversary of Paoli Massacre." *Daily Local News* (22 September 2002; 7 May 2004) <http://www.dailylocal.com/site/news.cfm?newsid=5456003&BRD=1671&PAG=461&dept_id+17782&rfi=6>.